The Lucky Numbers
Oracle

By the same author:

The Principles of Numerology

The Lucky Numbers Oracle

Discover the Power of Numerology

Sonia Ducie

Association Internationale
De Numerologues

Thorsons
An Imprint of HarperCollins*Publishers*

Thorsons
An Imprint of HarperCollins*Publishers*
77–85 Fulham Palace Road
Hammersmith, London W6 8JB

The Thorsons website address is: www.thorsons.com

Published by Thorsons 1999

1 3 5 7 9 10 8 6 4 2

A catalogue record for this book is
available from the British Library

ISBN 0 7225 3880 4

Printed and bound in Great Britain by
Woolnough Bookbinding, Irthlingborough, Northants

Contents

Part One

Introduction

What Is Numerology?

Numbers are fascinating even as black-and-white digits on a page – ask anybody who works with money or numbers on a daily basis and they will tell you how magnetic numbers are, how they draw you in. To a Numerologist, however, numbers are moving energies which reveal much more than their value to you. Their qualities, both positive and negative, and the potential they contain are constantly influencing you. Indeed, numbers form the basis of all life.

Numbers can teach you as much about the bigger picture as about your own life. Indeed, Numerology can be astonishingly revealing and provide you with the key to a deeper understanding of yourself and the universe. By observing some of the common characteristics of each number and allowing your intuition to do the rest, you will surely be convinced by Numerology.

Life flows to its own rhythm, and you have your own natural rhythm and cycles too. One way to observe this is on the dance floor – have you noticed how everyone expresses themselves differently in the way they move? People are dancing to their own rhythm even though they are collectively listening to the same music.

In Numerology life moves in cycles of 1 to 9. You can observe your natural cycles by applying Numerology to your date of birth and names (particularly the ones on your birth certificate). Each letter equates to a number which when totalled gives additional information about your life. From A to Z these add up from 1 to

26. For example A = 1, P = 7, H = 8, etc. (You can read further about this in my book *The Principles of Numerology*.)

History

Numbers are potent revealers of the truth, crystallizations of life and the universe. Throughout the ages many civilizations have recognized this. Each village or country once had its own scribes and sages who mapped out life according to numbers. The Greek philosopher Pythagoras held one such role and applied Numerology to find out more about the synchronicity of life and the universe. There were many before and after him. Indeed, anyone who possesses an enquiring mind and who is deeply in tune with life will usually have some understanding or awareness of numbers.

Today, Numerology is booming as more and more people realize its true potential and the value of this wonderful tool. There are many methods of Numerology and many ways to apply it to life, but the essential energy it contains, and the core messages it reveals, are always the same.

This Book is for You

In this book are 250 messages to feed your mind, body and spirit. Each message is based on the Numerology of the numbers for the heading it represents. So enjoy yourself and learn to be open to what the numbers reveal to you, both in the words on the page and 'between the lines', from your own inner intuition and knowledge.

How To Use This Book

There are many ways to use this book but the most important thing to remember is to use your intuition and inner wisdom to guide you. You can start at Message 1 and systematically work your way through. Perhaps you may read one message on one day, two or three the next day, and none for the rest of the week, and so on. You may also be tempted to simply open the book at random and read a message which synchronicity has picked out for you. Another method is to think of a situation and open up the book for a little light on the subject.

Numbers can jump out at you from all corners as you go about your daily life, and you can look these numbers up in this book (if they are between 1 and 250) to get a little taster of what they may be mirroring back to you at that time. For example, perhaps you go to work on the number 40 bus, or you sit in seat number 40 on the train; perhaps you are aged 40, and your house number is 40 too, and so on. So you can look up the number 40 in this book.

You will notice that each of the messages from 10 upwards is written with a single digit between 1 to 9 at the end; this is the culmination of the whole number added together. Everything in life is condensed into these single digits and the repeating nine cycles in nature.

Life is simple, and these messages can bring awareness of the simplicity in life. Enjoy *The Lucky Numbers Oracle* and be inspired to search for the truth in every area of your life using the fascinating tool of Numerology.

List Of Messages

Part Two

Messages

1

Live Life Fully

Every day is a new beginning, and each moment is a new opportunity to live life fully. When you begin a new journey it may seem awesome ... Which way do I go? What do I do? Who will accompany me on this new journey? Many questions may fill your mind, but it is only by living life and experiencing each moment – new, afresh – that your questions are answered and your life is revealed. You may want to compulsively jump or rush into things, but a little conscious thought given to potential actions may help you. You can use positive thoughts to consciously work *with* any changes in direction and to help you make the most of new opportunities which may come your way.

2

Find Inner Peace

You may feel that peace is a quality found by creating a peaceful environment. For example, by turning off the radio, television, or going into a quiet room where there are no people to talk to you. How is it, then, that when you are at home with children running around you, or with builders drilling a hole in the street next to your front door, that you at times are able to find a profound sense of peace? The answer lies within. Peace is only achieved by feeling peace within yourself and, for that moment, at peace within the world in which you live. Moments of inner peace enable you to feel complete and at one with your soul, and with life.

3

Feel Joy

When others are feeling low, spread a little sunshine in their lives by radiating your inner sense of joy. Joy is an inner state of being that allows you to feel free to express the light of your soul to the world. Radiating joy is one sure way to attract other joyous people to you – like attracts like – and together you can uplift and influence those who come into contact with you. Make way for joy, even on days when the clouds seem to hem you in and the darkness prevails; and remember that, like the sun which sometimes hides under the clouds, it is always there. Be open to joy in your life.

4

Be Practical

Being practical means being realistic about life, and being able to carry out necessary tasks in a realistic way. For example, if you know that you have an appointment at 5pm and that you need to cook dinner for 10 friends by 8pm, then remembering to buy the food beforehand, and perhaps employing the services of willing helpers, may help your day and evening run more smoothly. When you go through times of crisis, being practical and remembering to take responsibility for your practical daily needs may help you to survive and to get through them.

5

Dance Your Life Away

Dancing is one sure way of finding your own footing and getting in touch with your own rhythm in life. Everyone dances in their own unique way. Dancing is one way of expressing your inner self and your soul; it's fun to do, and getting down with those close to you is stimulating and one way to connect with them too. Dancing can help to lighten your load. By taking to the 'dance floor', even when at times it feels a great effort, and allowing your body to move how it wants to, you may be able to express how you feel and release stale energy. Dancing can lift your spirits and fill you with renewed vitality.

6

Open Your Heart

It is easy to open your heart when you are in love with a wonderful partner because life seems rosy and it feels good to open your heart to someone who makes you feel good. In reality, however, you feel good because you are in touch with the love inside you, and your lover is mirroring this feeling of love back to you. Love is always present in your heart and soul but at times you may close your heart to love, perhaps because you feel very sensitive and are afraid that you will get hurt. But love can also mend a broken heart and help you to love yourself again, and to love others. Love conquers all, and living life with an open heart full of love means that at times when you feel hurt you can still remain open to life and love.

7

Create Miracles In Your Life

A miracle is when the seemingly impossible happens, and things occur which take your breath away. Miracles are in effect simply laws of nature which indicate that you are in the right place at the right time, doing what you are meant to be doing; your mind, body and spirit are aligned. Miracles happen all the time but you may not recognize them or see them, even when they are placed in front of your very eyes. For example, your car which broke down in the middle of nowhere suddenly starts, even though you logically know it needs more fuel, and delivers you safely to your door. You are a part of nature, and accepting its power may be one way to appreciate all the miracles that occur in your life.

8

Be Successful

Trying to be successful is very different from *being* successful. The first requires energy to push something with great effort; the second happens effortlessly. Yes, you still need to do your homework if you are going to pass your exams, but simply being yourself and doing the best you can takes the effort out of trying as you relax into what you are doing, which can often bring even greater success. Real success often happens when you are not looking for it, when you are simply getting on with your day-to-day life and enjoying what you do. Whether in your career or in your relationships, allow your inner self – the real you – to shine through.

9

Find Ways To Disappear

When you are helping others or perhaps simply being with others you may feel as though you have disappeared, because you feel so connected with them that the 'little you' or your ego has temporarily gone. You may feel that you really fit in with people at these times or that you have found your place in life where you belong. These can be great moments of connection to others because you are truly connected to your inner self or spiritual self (which has not disappeared) and to life. At other times when you see yourself DOING something good for somebody just to get their attention, then your ego may scream out, 'let go and just BE you'. That is the real you, the inner you.

10/1

Flex Your Mind

At times, you may find your thoughts getting stuck in a rut. For example, there may be a specific problem to which you just can't seem to find a solution. It may help you to learn to flex your mind. Just as walking down the same street on the different side to which you would normally journey gives you a fresh view, then keeping an open mind also means new stimulus, new thoughts, new energy, and new ideas about life. Patterns of thoughts can keep you stuck in certain behaviour, and by learning to change your thoughts and adopt a positive attitude, you can change your life for the better. Being flexible helps to keep things flowing in your life too.

11/2

Be Inspired

To be inspired by life is to feel the wonder of the moment when something or someone catches your eye and connects you with your own inner light. When you are inspired you are open to life, and seeing a little bit more to life, and it may literally breathe fresh air and new energy into your mind, body and spirit. Little things may inspire you, like the way the sunlight reflects off a pond, or the moonlight reflects on your windowsill. Everyone is inspirational in their own way by possessing qualities and gifts which can inspire others. Inspiration can also drive us on to do better, to reach our goals, and ultimately to learn to simply be who we are, which can be the greatest inspiration of all.

12/3

Prepare A Lovely Meal

Whether you are preparing a meal for yourself, or for your partner, family or friends, preparing it with love can imbue the food with positive energy. Love energy is the most essential ingredient that can be added to food at any time – even when it's already on your plate! Indeed, if you enjoy preparing the table, the environment and the food, others can really sense this radiating through. Part of the preparation may be carefully considering what kind of foods may suit your mood that day, and what foods are ideal for your guests. You may even take the weather into consideration – hot soup on a steamy summer's day may not be ideal, for example. Preparing food with love and thought is one way of loving yourself and of showing others you care.

13/4

Transform Your Life

Every minute of your life, things are changing, and every moment is different from the last. Sometimes change happens and you are happy about the situations it brings, and at other times certain changes may be difficult to handle. Change enables you to grow, however, and you are constantly transforming. You can also change your life by the thoughts which influence the actions you take, and the situations in which you find yourself. You can also transform your life by choosing one career or partner rather than another. These are things which you can do something about. When things don't transform the way you want, look to see what this is teaching you, and learn to take responsibility for yourself.

14/5

Seek And You Shall Find

Knowledge is all around you – on the Internet, in films and books: you can gain knowledge by listening to a lecture, or by talking to people. However, by going inside yourself and communicating with your soul, your inner sense of knowing or knowledge is revealed. This knowledge may have been stored up from experiences you have learned about in the past. Indeed, your soul is communicating with you all the time, and by consciously listening to your inner self you may hear more clearly, and this may in turn help you to learn the lessons you need in life.

15/6

Make Wise Choices

You learn by experience. Making what you may classify as a mistake in one situation may mean that you become wise in similar situations a second time around. For example, perhaps you were asked to leave a study group because your continual lateness when turning up for class was disruptive for other students. You may rely on the wisdom of the situation and become brilliant at time-keeping in the future. Sometimes looking at the facts within a situation can help you to make wise choices too. In the above scenario, perhaps getting up early enough to allow yourself time to eat your breakfast and for your train journey to college may have been more thoughtful.

16/7

See Beauty In Life

When you walk down the street, do you notice the smiles on people's faces, beautiful flowers or trees, gorgeous dogs or fascinating things in shop windows? Or do you notice the cracks in the pavement, rubbish strewn about and frowning faces? Perhaps you notice both on different days or at different times. Being able to see the beauty in every single day, whatever the weather, is a gift, and a helpful one to cultivate. Indeed, beauty doesn't mean that life is always going to look or be perfect, but that life is as it is.

17/8

Find Your Inner Truth

When you find people in life who appear to have all the answers, you may try to adopt a little of their truth into your life in the hope that it will help you become more like them. For example, you work in an advertising agency and the high-flying Creative Director's truth is that 'people need to work 12 hours a day to be successful'. So you adopt a 12-hour day but more success doesn't seem to come your way. Perhaps your inner truth is telling you, 'if I get more sleep I can put seven good working hours into each day and become even more productive', and indeed your truth may bring even more success for you. Following your own inner truth is essential for you to be fully who you are, which is ultimately a prelude to success in any area of life.

18/9

Empower Yourself –
Empower Others

When you feel powerful it is because the power of spiritual energy is shining through you and helping you focus on a situation at hand, a goal or an intent. Power can be directed in a positive way to obtain positive results. It can also be used in a destructive way, by you throwing 'your' power around, telling people what to do, where to go, in order to get what you want. You can, however, utilize your sense of responsibility by using power wisely, and by empowering others to be powerful too. Perhaps you recognize that sometimes people need to feel comfortable with power, and by giving them a positive focus, such as a group goal in which to realize this, it may help them to handle power wisely.

19/1

Behave Yourself

In early childhood, patterns are set which largely determine your basic behaviour for the rest of your life, but by being conscious of the ways in which you behave you can work to release and change areas of conditioning. You also log into other people's behaviour, and this can influence you, particularly when you are around them. Every person is in your life in order to teach you some valuable lesson; the longer they are around the more you may need to learn from each other. However, everyone – including yourself – cannot always be on their best behaviour. In order to learn and move on with your life, the shadow side or your darker characteristics also need to be acknowledged. And then transformed into the light.

20/2

Life Is A Balancing Act

Life is a series of expansions and contractions. At times you are out in the world doing your thing, and at other times you may be reflective, quiet and inward looking (during these times it may even feel like nothing seems to be happening). However, both of these aspects are necessary in order to help you understand more about the balancing process in life. At times you may find yourself experiencing one aspect to the extreme, and like a pendulum you may swing from one side to the other. Perhaps you may be indifferent as to whether life takes you one way or another, or you may stay centred in the middle of things. Nature knows best and helps you to work your life out to ultimately bring balance into your life.

21/3

An Abundant Life

Abundance is a natural state that happens when you simply allow your life to flow in the direction in which it is meant to flow. If you have always loved mathematics then it may seem natural for you to study this subject deeply, or even take up a career as a statistician or accountant in adult life. Perhaps your love of numbers overflows, so that you attract an abundance of work to flow your way. Most people have an abundance of something in their lives. Do you have an abundance of love? money? sex? food? possessions? friends? family? or perhaps you travel in abundance? It may help you to be aware of the abundance you have right now, and to appreciate this – lucky you!

22/4

Find A Comfortable Spot

Getting comfortable with yourself is one way to ensure that you feel safe and comfortable with others. People may also feel your inner sense of security and feel at ease with you too. Uncomfortable situations do arise in life, perhaps situations in which you may not have found yourself before. If you feel comfortable within yourself, however, you may handle these situations more easily, and find yourself sailing through these potentially challenging times. Everyone has their own 'comfort zone', but breaking out of it from time to time and venturing into the unknown (even though this rattles your sense of security for a while) may also help you to grow.

23/5

Go Travelling

Travelling is an adventure. As you are transported by bus, train, car, ship and aeroplane around the world, you see different sights, are stimulated by different smells, eat different foods, witness different cultures. Hot climates one week, cold climates the next, with everything in between. Perhaps you travel no further than journeying around your local environment but this can still stimulate your senses and become an adventure too. However, you can also journey into your mind or soul, delve deep inside to find out more about yourself and the ways of the world. Once you have travelled the world, what more is there to see ... but the inward journey is never ending and goes on to eternity.

24/6

Guilt Is A Trip

Some people get off on guilt: 'Oh I feel terrible that I didn't do this or that, it's all my fault'. Feeling guilty is useful at times, in order, for example, to teach you a lesson about something you have done which was not in integrity. At these times it can encourage you to take positive actions so that you do not repeat the situation. However, sometimes people wallow in guilt to get attention, for others to feel sorry for them, and sometimes the guilt simply compounds itself. Wallowing in guilt is a trip away from your soul; it is a little dance around an issue, where you are preventing yourself from learning what it is you need and then letting these feelings go. A little self-forgiveness at these times can go a long way.

25/7

It's Your Lucky Day!

As you travel through life, learning your lessons along the way, sometimes it is helpful to simply stop and appreciate today – you're alive now, it's your lucky day! Perhaps you can appreciate good health, loving people around you, your home, your cat or dog, and indeed everything in your life today. Appreciation is a way of giving back something to the universe which created you. Have you ever thought of saying 'thank you' to your parents for having you? Sounds daft, but where would you have been without them? Life slips by, and appreciating each day as something special means that you may be able to make the most out of opportunities which come your way.

26/8

Love Your Inner Child

Young children are so open. They speak when they want to, scream and shout too, and feel free to tell you what they think of you. Everyone has an inner child, that space inside you which feels vulnerable sometimes, or at other times feels safe to express what is inside you. Perhaps you ignore or criticize your inner child – 'No you can't have or do this or that' – and keep that part of you locked away. However, allowing your inner child out to play sometimes can be fun, and learning to love your inner child and to listen to what he or she needs to communicate may also be essential for you to be truly comfortable within yourself. If someone knocks, it is only by opening the door that you find out what they need.

27/9

Learn To Meditate

In the fast-paced world in which we live, many people are learning simple meditation techniques to help them reconnect to their inner self, and feel connected to others too. Meditation may seem a little mysterious (there are many different methods from chanting, walking, breathing to visualization) but meditation is something which is also done naturally. For example, when you are baking or working you may meditate – that is simply slip into another realm of consciousness by drawing upon your resources from deep within. You may also meditate when you stare at a beautiful painting or one which provokes you to introspection. However, recognizing when you need to spend a few minutes meditating and setting aside time to do so may also be helpful.

28/1

Go For Life

It is one thing to sit thinking about all the wonderful ideas you may have floating around your head, but procrastinating about doing something about them isn't going to help you or anyone. Why not go for what feels right for you to do right now? Going for what you want may not always bring you instant results, but as sure as grass is green, it is going to make you feel better knowing that you took some actions to materialize your goals into reality. Today may be just the right time for you to go for life fully, with no regrets and great lessons to be learned along the way, whatever the results.

29/2

Find Your Soul Mate

Who is your Soul Mate? Where is he or she right now? How do you find that special one? The answer is that your Soul Mate is here with you right now – your Soul Mate is you, that soul connection deep inside you. Your Soul Mate is your best friend, your closest ally, your nearest and dearest, and is like a lover who spares no expense when it comes to being intimate with you. That is your soul or inner essence which travels every moment of your life's journey with you, dancing by your side – indeed your soul can lead you if you choose. Of course you can also find Soul Mates outside yourself, people with whom you feel intrinsically connected. These relationships mirror the deep connection your body has with the Soul aspect within you.

30/3

Learn To Laugh

It is often said that laughter is the best medicine, and this has indeed been medically proven in many corners of the globe. In some places you can even attend a Laughter Clinic or take Clowning Therapy where good fun is the order of the day. Laughter lightens the atmosphere and helps problems simply disappear into thin air, for a while anyway. Cultivating the quality of humour can therefore be only a positive action to take. Perhaps today you can tell a joke and uplift those around you, or choose to let go of worrying about a problem by looking at the funny side of life, and who knows, it may even help to improve your health along the way.

31/4

Shine Your Light

Light is the source from which we all come – sunlight supports all life: animal, mineral, human and even the unseen worlds around us. Light is who you really are; it is the essence of your very being; and it is to the light that you always return. Today, connect with your inner light, your spiritual will, and allow it to drive you forwards to do those things which your soul directs you to do. Perhaps your soul is asking you to communicate clearly to the world so that others can connect with you clearly too, or it may be asking you to learn to give a little more to those around you, and so on. Allow yourself to bathe in this inner light and you may indeed find a sense of renewal and strength which helps you go on with your life.

32/5

Train Your Brain

Your brain is a muscle that needs exercising mentally in order to keep it fit, just like your physical body needs exercise to keep it supple and flexible. Giving your brain a good workout can help keep you balanced, because your thoughts influence your actions, which influence your whole mind, body and spirit. When you were young, at school, learning helped to keep your active mind stimulated with facts, figures and ideas, but it is important to keep on learning too. Many people do crosswords, go on the internet, or continue studying at night school or college. Working out problems can be another way of keeping your brain active, and listening to people is a good way to stimulate your mind too.

33/6

Heal Old Hurts

Every day is an opportunity to heal some part of you which needs to be brought into wholeness, and it is only by becoming conscious of ways in which you hurt that you can really heal those parts of yourself. You may be jealous of a friend, for example, and perhaps by looking at your inner landscape you can discover why you feel this way. You may realize that it is nothing to do with your friend at all. Feelings and emotions are transient but they do help reveal deeper aspects of ourselves which may need to be addressed. You may also find it helpful to look at the bigger picture when you are angry, sad, or upset, so that you can see everyone's needs – you may even feel better instantaneously.

34/7

Trust The Process

Life is a process of events which are constantly unfolding. Sometimes you may stop and question this process because you want life to be different. Perhaps you want something which you haven't got and think you 'should' have it. Everything in life is there to teach you some essential lessons, however, and by accepting them as best you can and learning the lessons they are teaching you, then you can move on. The process of life is an unfolding story. Think how your book will look by the end of your life: some interesting bits, some highs, some lows, and out of it all there are the lessons you learned along the way.

35/8

Find Stillness

When your soul has been working hard you may need a rest for a moment to be in stillness. This will enable you to see where you have come from, where you are right now, and in what direction you may need to head off next. It may seem a bit like the moment of death, when events of your lifetime are flooded before your very eyes, and when your mind may catch a glimpse of your next lifetime before you consciously leave your physical body. A moment of stillness. When you stand still it may feel as though nothing is happening, but this space allows for much transformation and change. Stillness is therefore an essential part of the day.

36/9

Detachment

When you are detached you can take part in your life much easier than when you attach yourself to specific outcomes in your relationships, career or ambitions. For example, when you are attached to getting promotion at work you may overwork in order to 'prove' yourself, and hence your health, your social and personal life may all suffer. Even when you are not at work you may be constantly thinking of your work, or ways in which you can get the golden fleece. When one part of you is tightly holding on, it prevents your whole energy system from flowing with ease. Being detached can free up this energy; indeed your goals may flow your way more easily at these times.

37/1

Learn To Visualize

Everyone visualizes all the time. For example, you are working and are already visualizing the cream cake you want to eat for lunch, or your evening's date with your new flame. Seeing or visualizing something in your mind's eye may actually help you to create that very thing because you are throwing out your thoughts and intentions (your energy) towards this situation. You also need to learn to take responsibility for your visions/thoughts because they are very powerful. One wonderful way to use creative visualization is within a group where you can use it positively to help others, and where used collectively it becomes more potent. For example, a group may visualize a positive outcome to a world conflict, and so on.

38/2

Rise To The Occasion

When circumstances arise in your life which require you to give a little bit more, do you back away and say 'No thank you', or do you rise to the occasion and say 'I can handle this' as you delve into the unknown? Of course it is your choice; you are responsible for your own thoughts and actions; but breaking through into unknown territory can also mean a breakthrough in your own life as challenging situations help you to grow. Today, be aware of areas where you back down or choose to face what comes your way with a positive attitude as you say 'I can do it'. There is no right or wrong way; both paths can teach you more about yourself and about life.

39/3

Jump For Joy

At times you may amble through life effortlessly, meandering this way and that, taking time to stop off and sight-see occasionally, and resting under the moon or in the sunshine during other times. Today, however, life is asking you to jump for joy; life is like a holiday where you can experience all the good things in life. Yes, tears and tribulations may also come your way but learning to view even those with a positive mind can help you to make the most of your life. What do you normally do on holiday – eat especially nice foods, dance all night, become wonderfully romantic, become more energetic or lighter in spirit? Remember that you do not need to go away on holiday to do these things; you can incorporate them into your life here today … then life really can become a holiday.

40/4

Make A Shopping List

One lifetime is like a shopping list – you tick some things off your long list as you don't manage to locate everything you need in one go. You save the other things on your list for your next trip in your next lifetime. Shopping lists are very helpful, however, because you nearly always manage to return home with the essential things at the top of the list. Remember that at any time you can change your list by adding new items in and taking old items away, particularly if you no longer need them (you didn't need the chocolate cake after all). Sometimes when you go shopping, one item takes longer to find than others, but like life, you feel really wonderful when you eventually tick that thing off your list – done!

41/5

Be Free

Everyone is essentially free because nobody can own your soul. It is good to remember this, particularly at times when you may feel trapped and hemmed in by life and responsibilities. For example, you may feel that your partner is often possessive about you. In return, you may want to pull away and feel like wandering off, or simply retaliate verbally, and so on. It may help you to realize that they couldn't possibly own you – the real you, your soul. However, in some way you have contributed to creating the situation you are in – relationships are two-way mirrors – but realizing that you are both free can be very liberating for both of you.

42/6

Get Motivated

Motivation comes from your emotions; have you ever noticed that when you are in love and feeling good you have much more energy to devote to your life? Or at times when you feel low it is much more difficult to get up and take the dog for a walk – it just feels like too much effort? At these times making a little effort to do something can jump-start your engine and get you back into the swing of things. For example, you are tired at the end of the day and don't feel like attending your aerobics class but afterwards you are buzzing with energy and ready to go. Life is like that too; sometimes a little effort at first means a less strenuous time later on.

43/7

Degeneration

Degeneration is useful; food thrown onto a compost heap breaks down and enriches the soil, which in turn nourishes food grown there which when eaten supplies you with vital nutrients and energy. This constant recycling of nature helps us to grow. In life, times of degeneration are necessary because they enable you to break down outmoded patterns of behaviour so that you can build up new positive patterns which can continue to support you in your growth. Degeneration feels like an uncomfortable process but if you go with the changes, the process may become easier in some way. In effect, degeneration is happening all the time in the body because cells and their memories are constantly dying and being renewed, even though you are consciously unaware of this process.

44/8

Be A Guide

If you were a Girl Guide or a Boy Scout when you were a child then you may have been taught to think of the community and ways in which you can help those around you, or guide others in a positive way. We are each other's guides, and lead others in some way. For example, you may be brilliant at directing others (perhaps you use this quality particularly at work), and you may attract people who need to learn about this quality from you. In return, you may need to learn from them how to be more laid back, and instead of always directing others, learn to allow life to direct you instead. Sometimes one person can guide many people at once, such as an elected politician, a doctor, a parent, and so on. Today, learn to take responsibility for the way in which you guide others.

45/9

Share A Passion

What is your passion? Singing, dancing, talking, playing a musical instrument, painting, cooking, gardening, working? There are so many from which you can choose. Passions are wonderful teachers because they connect you with your gifts and your inner self which guides you to use them. When you have a passion you can light up others' lives with it too. Perhaps someone can share their passion for pottery with you (it may even encourage you to give it a go), or you can share your passion for antiques by giving a public lecture. When you have a passion it feeds all other areas of your life as mind, body and spirit are connected, and it can make you feel more alive.

46/1

Dedication

When you find something of great interest to you then you may choose to dedicate some or much of your time to exploring it. For example, you may enjoy nursing and looking after others. When you find an interest that captures your attention almost to the exclusion of everything else (be it for an afternoon, week, or even longer), it may be your soul connecting with you at a very deep level and drawing it to your attention. Finding some time for your true interests may enrich your life, and may even lead you towards a completely new direction in your career, for example.

47/2

Create A Little Magic

If today you find yourself staring into thin air dreaming, then perhaps you may like to write down what it is you were dreaming about and to ponder upon this for a while. In life, some dreams can and do become reality, whilst others merely stay floating around in your mind. For example, perhaps you dream of living in a hot country with little rain, as you live near the sea in a cold climate where downpours are regular occurrences. One day you decide to take some positive action to help you materialize this dream; you apply for a position in Hawaii. You sail through the interview, get the job and only one month later there you are, living in hot and sunny climes. Knowing what your dreams are is one essential ingredient to success.

48/3

Discipline Helps

When you are learning to balance many different aspects of your life, a little discipline can go a long way. Discipline helps the ship to run more smoothly because it irons out potential difficulties. For example, if you know that you need to finish a project for a client, help your parents move house and attend a parents' meeting at your children's school, all around the same time, then being disciplined about how much time you can afford to give to each may really help. Of course, the unexpected does happen in life and your needs may change – perhaps your client needs the project finished sooner, and so on. Being adaptable to change whilst being disciplined about things you need to do may really help you manage your life.

49/4

Dramas Are Tests

Dramas often occur: you lose your front door keys and lock yourself out; a friend is rushed to hospital and you are asked to take care of their child; you have to change trains on the way home because the one you are on breaks down, and so on. But these things are all part of life and you don't need to make them into dramas at all, although at times it may be a challenge not to do so. Dramas are tests – they test your strength, your ability to remain calm when things fall apart, and your ability to carry on. Sometimes, seeing past the drama to the lesson that life is trying to teach you can be really useful.

50/5

Be Spontaneous

When situations feel stuck in a rut, adding a little spark of spontaneity to your life may really help to move things along. For example, you have been dating a new lover for over seven months, and although your sex life was exciting when you first met, it now seems to have settled down into a dull routine. You may spontaneously suggest to your lover that you make love in a different position, or outdoors, and so on, next time around. Perhaps you spontaneously wear something really sexy or dress out of character on your next date. Of course, what is spice to one person is coals to another, so you may like to find out what your lover likes too!

51/6

Giving Birth

As you travel through your life you experience a myriad of different feelings, but each time you feel a strong emotion it may feel like you are giving birth to something new. 'I have never felt such … joy, sadness, frustration, anger,' you may exclaim to those around you. Yet you probably have experienced those emotions before, albeit in different circumstances. Anger is anger, sadness is sadness, and so on. However, you may at some point find yourself going so deep into one emotion that there seems nowhere left to go. This purification of your emotions may indeed feel like you are giving birth, but it may eventually help guide you to a feeling of wholeness.

52/7

Be Vulnerable

You may believe that being emotionally vulnerable is a weakness because you feel the need to protect yourself from the world, or feel that if you are vulnerable somebody will hurt you. Being emotionally vulnerable, however, means that you are open to life. This can be a good thing because the more life you can allow into your mind, body and spirit, the more you can feel truly alive. Being vulnerable puts you in receiving mode, for when you are closed down nothing can get through your doors. There are times when you may feel safe to be vulnerable, such as with a lover or a family member, and other times when you do not. You choose times when it feels right for you.

53/8

Take Control

Control is often frowned upon as being something negative, but somebody has to take control in life, and that person may be you. Indeed, everyone needs to learn to take control, or take responsibility for their own lives. You can make your life work by getting up and doing something about it rather than being like a casual bystander at the races who happily watches life speed past – and the race is over in a flash. Taking control may not come easily, but once you begin to flex this muscle it can get easier and you may even enjoy it.

54/9

Be Daring

You don't need to climb Mount Everest or ride a bicycle across the Sahara desert to be daring. You simply need to be able to do or say something which pushes you a little past your regular comfort zone. Perhaps you find yourself daring to spend more money on yourself at the hairdressers for example, or daring yourself to ring up that person of your dreams and ask him or her out on a date. You may dare yourself to invite the vicar for Sunday lunch with your family, although you may be more surprised when the vicar's response is 'Yes please'. Sometimes dares may backfire on you, particularly if you dare to do something which is harmful to others; it may be helpful to think before you act. However, dares mean that you are willing to take a chance on life which may be just the tonic you need.

55/1

Sing A Song

Sing a song and angels sing with you. It doesn't matter if you can't sing in tune; learning to express yourself through sound is a wonderful way to pass the time. When you sing you release stored up energy and connect with your mind and emotions. Have you ever found yourself crying with joy because your song has touched some part deep inside? This is because you have contacted your soul. Perhaps you enjoy playing some music and singing along with that too, and you may love to sing in beautiful harmonies. You may even take this one step further and decide to take up singing lessons with a professional which may bring even more joy and happiness into your life.

56/2

Consistency

In order to be consistent in your behaviour or attitude, it means that on some level you have made commitments in your life. For example, you may be consistently reliable at work: you always turn up on time, you always deliver the work you say you'll do, and so on. You may also be consistently unreliable with your partner in some way. Sometimes when business employers look at your CV they may see that you have worked consistently for one company, or in one field, for a long time, and this may encourage them to employ you. If you are being interviewed for your first job, then they may recognize this potential quality within you too. Being consistent can at times benefit you and all those in your life.

57/3

Learn To Focus

Focusing is an art form which comes easily to some people and is a complete mystery to others. Focusing is simply the ability to direct all your thoughts and energy on something for a specific amount of time. Have you noticed that when you really want something you seem to focus much of your thoughts and your energy towards this goal? You may also find that it is easier to focus on things you love doing. Or perhaps you are able to focus on things which need to be done, even if you don't like doing them, like the washing up which has piled up in the sink, for example. It is often said that successful people are those who continually focus on their goals and visions. Today, notice what you choose to focus your attention on.

58/4

Rebirth

Life is constantly renewing itself; each day is a new beginning, each sunset is an ending, and everything in between is but an opportunity for growth. Growth is systematic; it happens naturally. If you miss an opportunity that comes your way one day it will never return in exactly the same way because you are constantly changing. Tomorrow you will be different from how you are today in some way, simply from having experienced another day. As you get to the end of this day it may be useful to review what you have learned or what you have achieved with your day, and to say 'thank you'.

59/5

Have A Party

Life's one big party and there are so many people in the world taking part all at once. Of course, some parties you enjoy more than others. For example, there may be times when you feel like switching off and going to sit by yourself in the corner because you're tired, or you want a rest from the dance floor. Perhaps you want to leave the party because the music's too loud, or because you ate too much and feel ill. Maybe you find the guests boring, or you end up talking with someone all evening about some amazing subject or shimmy away with them into the night. However, this world party has room for everyone, which gives you plenty of choice for party company.

60/6

Life Is A Luxury

Every time you feel low, remember that this is a big, wide world to which you belong and that you have been allowed the luxury to experience life on earth. If you are healthy it is your biggest luxury; if you have all the things you need to survive then that is another luxury, along with the love and warmth of close ones. Therefore, all the things you may think of as luxuries now are in effect 'extras' – a visit to the cinema, owning a car, travelling around the world, having the company of wonderful animals around your home, and so on. Notice what luxuries you have in your life, and what are 'extras' – see what you've got and how fortunate you are.

61/7

Look For Goodness

It is easy to feel dishevelled and battered by life at times when everything seems to be going 'wrong'. For example, you may feel defeated by losing your job, going to the dentist for treatment, or ending a relationship, perhaps all in the same day. 'What a life' you may think. But it is at these exact times when it can help you to look for the goodness in people, in life and, most importantly, within yourself, because it is always there. Indeed, at these times you may blame yourself for being a 'bad' person, but by being caring towards yourself you open up the door to allow others to get close to you and to love and care for you too. Today look for the goodness in life.

62/8

Lose Your Status

From a soul's perspective, status doesn't exist because all souls are equal and have no need for classification. It is only when you come down to earthly terms that status becomes a word for you to watch out for. Like being a Managing Director of a company may seem like status to some, or owning lots of money may seem like status to others. Are you a Mr, Miss, Mrs or Ms? These 'status symbols' seem to follow us around, and there may seem to be no escape from them. You may at times want to assume certain status because it makes you feel in control, the best, and perhaps it gives you some kind of false security. However, losing your desire for status (even if you are bestowed with it by others) may be useful because then you can recognize your true self – your soul.

63/9

Find Time For Compliments

When you have done a good job at work and your boss congratulates you, how do you react? Do you say 'Oh it was nothing!' or 'I could have done better', and so on, or do you say 'Thanks', and think 'I deserve that because I did do well'? Celebrating life is important because it welcomes more love and potentially more success into your life. By giving a positive response when somebody praises you, then they are receiving positive energy too. You can also give compliments to people, such as, 'I like your hair', 'Dinner was delicious' and so on, and in this way you are sending out even more positive energy. A life without compliments would be dull, so learn to show a little appreciation to others and appreciate the compliments which come your way.

64/1

Find Something New

Sometimes it may seem that each day is just blending into the next with nothing new happening: the telephone hardly rings, the postman turns up empty-handed, and even your newsagent forgets to say 'Good morning'. You may go to the same desk at the same job you have been in for 14 years and sit with the same group of people. However, the newspapers carry different stories from one day to the next and you may find some interesting topics. Perhaps you can buy a different paper to your regular one, or buy a magazine which you may not normally consider. Each day, people are different too; their moods, clothes and their conversations can change. Today, find something new about your day. You can also take actions to create new things in your life if you choose.

65/2

Communicate Your Wisdom

Have you heard the saying 'Wise to the occasion'? This means that you have learned something from past experience which you can apply the next time you find yourself in a similar situation. For example, you may be mean with your money, and when buying a house you refuse to pay for a surveyor to check out the condition of the property. Six months into your new home the roof leaks, and you realize that there is damp in the kitchen. Next time you buy a house your inner wisdom may tell you to spare no expense when employing a reliable surveyor. Learning to listen to your inner wisdom may really help your life run more smoothly at times, but when you don't follow it you can learn valuable lessons too.

66/3

Generosity

Some people are very generous with their love – because it makes them feel good, and they gain pleasure from knowing that others feel loved too. The reason they can give so much is because they feel an immense welling up of love in their heart and their cup simply overflows, which is then relayed on to others in a loving exchange. They may also be generous with money or their possessions, because these things are also an expression of the love energy they feel. Today, be aware of allowing your heart to fill with love; you can also choose to be generous with your love and to allow in the generosity of others, whether that be on the physical, emotional, mental or spiritual levels.

67/4

Healing

You may think of healing as something grand; perhaps you visualize a healer, complementary therapist or doctor healing you with various techniques or medicines. However, you are healing all the time. That is because you learn something new each day. Each day a little healing takes place. For example, if one of your major lessons in life is learning how to communicate, then perhaps your partner, children, work colleagues and animals may be helping you learn this lesson on a daily basis. One day you may suddenly wake up and realize that now you can communicate really well but there is always more refining of this lesson to do. Today, become aware of ways in which you are healing yourself and others.

68/5

Buy Some Flowers

Flowers reflect your mood; you may buy enormous red daisies, serene white lilies, lively geraniums or a bunch of colourful carnations, perhaps even a single stem of some exotic flower too. Flowers for a special occasion, for your lover or loved one, flowers to cheer you up because you've had a miserable day, flowers for a funeral, or you may like to buy flowers for no reason other than appreciating the splendid beauty of nature. Perhaps you grow flowers in your garden, nurturing them and watching them grow, and eventually die. Flowers may reflect your inner beauty, and having flowers around you can help to bring energy and vitality into your life. Flowers really do say it all.

69/6

Sensuality

We are all sensual beings because we feel our way through life with the five senses we possess: we smell perfumes; we see the world around us; we touch and are touched by people; we can hear glorious sounds; and we taste delicious foods. Most of us are lucky enough to possess all five senses, which enable us to relate to the world. However, you also have a sixth sense, your instinct, which is your ability to be able to sense others. Some people call this psychic energy. For example, you may get a 'hunch' that your train is going to be delayed so you leave home later than normal, only to find your train indeed arrives 15 minutes late. Today enjoy sensuality.

70/7

Be Patient

Patience is a gift and it is also a quality which you can cultivate to help you make the most out of your life. When you are impatient you may miss out on experiencing your life fully. For example, if you hurry your children to school you may lose an extra five minutes with your children, or extra time with your partner in the morning when you could be cuddling up in bed. Impatience happens when you are focusing on the next moment instead of focusing on the current one. Life has its own rhythm and so do you, and allowing your body to live life according to its own rhythm and time can help to take the pressure off you.

71/8

Relentlessness

When you have a specific goal which you are aiming for, particularly if it is something which can help others, then you may find that your drive turns into relentless determination to carry the job through. This may mean, for example, that you are able to go on and on, and even when challenges come your way which may try to take you off course, you still succeed in carrying on towards your goals. Sometimes relentlessness can come across as ruthlessness as you may be uncaring about whom you trundle over to get to your goals. However, true relentlessness is far from harmful to others as it can uplift and inspire them so that they may exude some positive energy too.

72/9

You Are A Specialist

Everyone is good at something and has their own little speciality and unique way of doing something or way of being. For example, you may be a specialist at massage and have mastered your own specific technique, or be a specialist at icing cakes which everyone appreciates. Perhaps you are a specialist at making others laugh, and so on. Indeed, you don't need to be a fine artist who restores 'Old Masters' from art galleries around the world to be considered a specialist – you are one right now. Today, be aware of your specialities which are your gifts; you can, of course, find new things to specialize in at any time during your life.

73/1

Listen To Intuition

Intuition can sometimes seem like an inner voice which transmits itself through your mind. More commonly, when intuition presents itself it appears as a sense of 'knowing'. For example, you receive the news that you have passed your exams, and you say, 'I just knew that I would'. Sometimes you may ignore this sense of knowing because your logical brain questions it, and because it is much more difficult to trust something which can't be proved at the time. If you do listen to the guiding messages of your intuition, it is sometimes helpful to use your logical brain to think things through before you make any decisions or take any actions. Intuition is actually an everyday tool which can be used practically, not only to help yourself, but also to help guide others.

74/2

Learn To Listen

When you listen to a friend talking, in a busy street for example, there are many sounds which you can hear: their voice, cars, the sounds of engines, other people talking, the wind or rain, and so on. But how much attention can you give to any one of these things – do you hear each of them or do they all blend into one? When you are talking to your friend you may indeed be focusing so intently that all the other sounds simply disappear, but if you focus on the sound of a car, for example, you may not hear what your friend is saying. Listening is a gift, and by truly listening to yourself and what is in your environment you can then respond in your own true way.

75/3

Be Quiet

When you come through periods of deep introspection and times of solitude life may seem to suddenly speed up. This may be because by being 'quiet' within yourself for a while you have created space for things to move, and only when you bring yourself back to your regular routine do you notice that things have changed or moved on. Sometimes problems may even resolve themselves during this period too. For example, perhaps you have had an argument with your ex-husband about who takes the children out at the weekend. By going deep within yourself, and simply by giving space to problems, they can at times resolve themselves in their own way, and for the best of all concerned.

76/4

Group Needs

Your needs are very important and it is your personal responsibility to look after them. However, you also belong to a group – for example, a family group, a work group, and of course you belong within a country or community group too. Each group has its own collective needs and you may be able to contribute towards them if you choose. For example, you may work in a community centre which desperately needs a new minibus. Perhaps you take on this group responsibility and organize lots of events to help raise enough money to provide this group need. However, there are many ways in which you may choose to help your group.

77/5

Your First Commitment

Commitments are necessary to enable you to get through life with ease. For example, you may commit to meeting your partner at a certain time in the evening, but what follows afterwards is largely dependent upon you getting together in the first place. Therefore, if you wish to build any kind of relationship or career then you can see that commitment is essential. In order for you to be able to make commitments then you need to be able to recognize what it is that you wish to commit to. This may take some soul-searching in certain situations, or the answer may come to you easily. However, your first commitment is always to yourself; it is up to you to make the most out of your own life by committing to making it work.

78/6

Your Best Friend

You are your own best friend because you are always there with yourself, night and day, and you know yourself intimately. This may sound strange, but making friends with yourself can help you to find inner peace. For example, you may be angry with yourself that you failed your exam and perhaps for a time you really hate yourself for it. However, life is there to teach you lessons and loving yourself for the 'mistakes' you make means that you can let go of them and move on. Some people talk to themselves, and this may sound peculiar, but it may be one good way to hear yourself think. Perhaps you can learn to talk to yourself with loving kindness, as though you were talking to your best friend.

79/7

Completion

You know that point when you have enjoyed a sumptuous dinner with friends and family; the final person has put down their glass and now you have all finished your meal; everyone is complete. The next part of the evening may be filled with conversation, music and action, and then you leave your family's house feeling complete. Or do you? Perhaps there was something more you wanted to discuss with your sister, and you didn't finish your conversation with Uncle Paul, and so on. This situation may be reminding you to look carefully at how you go about your daily life, because unfinished business can come back to you in the future for you to complete.

80/8

Karmic Ties

Karmic ties are like knots in a handkerchief which are difficult to get out – you pick at them but they are so tightly entwined that you don't seem to get very far very fast. Sometimes when you remove the knots they rematerialize and you have to start all over again. Karmic ties between people are very strong because they have built up from the relationships you may have had in many lifetimes together. Imagine if you have been married over and over again, all that you have been through together – no wonder the knots are binding. However, karmic relationships are extremely powerful; they can be the most potent teachers in your life, and you can learn many wonderful lessons from them.

81/9

Leadership

The best leaders are those who lead without thinking that they are the leader, and they may not even notice that they are leading. For example, the lead speaker at a discussion may be so involved with examining the topic of conversation with his or her colleagues that they do not even realize that it is they who are in charge of the crowd – or recognize their natural leadership ability to draw people out and encourage them to speak. Perhaps the group leader even thinks that it is the group which is leading them, and this may at times be so. However, knowing who the leader is, on a mountain trek for example, can be helpful because you know who to follow, although at times another person can always take the lead.

82/1

Victims

Being a victim to life means that you feel that there is nothing you can do to change the situation you are in for the better. However, you do have the choice about what attitude to take towards any painful situations you are in. That is, you can choose to take all your inner strength and look deeper at your immediate circumstances to see what lessons they may be teaching you. Perhaps you may even enjoy wallowing in being a victim because it gets you lots of attention: 'Oh poor me, the visit to the dentist was awful', instead of resting or taking a painkiller to help you deal with the problem. Most people experience being a victim at some point, but these can be valuable times for your personal development and growth in the long run.

83/2

Be Magnetic

You may think that there are general stereotypes about what is considered beautiful, sexy, attractive, and about what it is that turns people on. Looks certainly play a part – but it is the inner magnetism which actually draws people in and keeps them coming back for more. For example, have you ever noticed the look in, say, a supermodel's or actor's eyes? They are usually bright, alert and alive, with a sparkle that could light up a Christmas tree at night. This energy radiates out from the inside; it is the life-force saying 'I'm here', which is of course the inner spiritual light. You may feel 'animal magnetism' towards somebody based on your instincts of how they physically turn you on, but magnetism shines from within, and the eyes can be very revealing.

84/3

Growing Pains

Growing pains occur because you are changing. One part of you is still holding on for dear life while the other part is letting go and saying 'let's get on with this, I want to move forwards'. Growing pains can occur on any level – physical, emotional, mental and spiritual – and at any time; it's not just teenagers who get them. On the physical level, for example, you may experience pain which is associated with a real illness, like influenza, which has been medically diagnosed; but although this physical level is suffering, your spiritual level may be growing enormously. Growing pains are a natural part of life and at times they may get easier if you allow yourself to accept what's going on, if you can.

85/4

The Earth Moves

The Earth is moving all the time as it spins and turns, making its way around the sun, and if you were to hold a giant pendulum you would see this movement reflected as the pendulum swings back and forth. It makes sense, then, that if the Earth is constantly moving then so are you, even though you are not aware of it. Sometimes parts of the Earth's crust move and cause conflicts within surrounding areas, and likewise you may at times also experience conflicts in your life. When the Earth has readjusted itself it becomes stable again, for a while, like the calm after the storm which you may experience when (inner) conflicts are resolved. But remember that life on Earth is in a constant state of change, as the pendulum swings back and forth, and so are you.

86/5

Lighten Up

As you go through life you may at times feel like you are getting heavier and more burdened down with responsibilities, and your body may even reflect this as you walk around with your head hanging heavily towards the ground. You can, however, change your attitude towards the situation – learn to stop taking life so seriously, have some fun and games and lighten up. Perhaps in the middle of a heavy business meeting you suddenly think of something which makes you laugh to yourself, or you may decide to plan a weekend away with a loved one to help you forget about your heavy responsibilities for a while. There are many things you can do, but learning to laugh instead of cry at times when your life is bursting at the seams may really help.

87/6

Talent Spotter

Imagine if you were a professional talent spotter; you would be paid to go out every day and look for talent in the street and in parks, in restaurants, bars and night-clubs. Perhaps your job would be to look for an undiscovered talented artist, or to find a talented musician or singer for a band. When you look hard enough for some specific quality or talent, there is every chance that you will succeed – after all, your job depends upon it. In everyday life, talents jump out from everywhere. But how do you recognize your own talents? You become your own talent spotter of course. When you have found your inner talents then you can learn to develop them or simply use what's there, if you choose.

88/7

The Strong Silent Type

Even if you are the most bubbly person in the world it may help you to learn how to become the strong silent type for a while. This does not mean that you cannot speak, or do not want to speak, but simply that you are able to be quiet within yourself. Connecting with your inner self can help to centre you so that instead of talking incessantly or superficially, you are able to really connect with what it is you are saying. Perhaps you have already discovered that moments of connecting with your inner strength and stillness can help you in the material world. Eventually, you may be able to easily balance time spent introspecting and time spent bubbling over with energy, activity and communication.

89/8

Find Your Feet

At times in your life you may feel very sure of yourself; you feel in control, you know in which direction you are heading and you feel good. At these times you may feel strong about who you are, and trust that life is taking you along the right path. However, an event may turn up which turns you inwards, or makes you re-evaluate your life, such as a death, a divorce, a problem at work, and so on. Perhaps you don't feel as sure-footed as you once did and you take the knocks quite hard. At these times you may realize that whatever anyone says or does to try to help you, it is up to you to find your own inner strength and to find your own feet in order to carry on with your life. However, by walking a step at a time the rest follows.

90/9

Learn To Relax

You may have very high standards and expectations about your life; sometimes this can contribute towards putting pressure on yourself when there's no need. For example, perhaps you work 12 hours a day because you don't wish to let your customers down. However, you may be so tired that eventually you may be forced to slow down. Relaxation is essential; sleep is one way to relax, but you may also relax by reading, making love, having a massage, going for a walk, meditating, and so on. Indeed, anything which helps you to unwind and enables you to let go of thinking about things too deeply is wonderful for relaxation. It can help you to approach life with renewed energy and vitality again.

91/1

Learn To Drive

Life is like learning to drive; just when you think you've got there and perfected all your moves, a situation presents itself along your path and challenges your skills and all that you have learned. At times you drive along in your car happily and contentedly, enjoying the journey, and at other times you may want your driving instructor to see you out of a manoeuvre which you can't quite manage; you want him or her to take responsibility for you. Sometimes, as a learner driver, you may create hazards for others along your path, which requires you all to bring your attention to the present moment. Perhaps you were too busy looking out of the back window – at your past. Notice ways in which you influence others with the path you choose and how they influence you too.

92/2

Discover Your Own Morals

Morals are simply judgements about how you think people should live their lives. You have your own set of morals developed in your childhood but as you get older your morals may change. For example, as a child you may have been taught that when you send friends party invitations, they should reply. As an adult, you may be aware that friends may intend to come but are unable to reply. Perhaps they are away travelling or are ill. Your morals may now say that they still have manners but are simply being human. Sometimes it is also helpful to look at the bigger picture instead of judging others by your own morals.

93/3

Listen To Some Music

Music can influence you in many different ways; it can lift you up when you are feeling low, stimulate you into action when you are feeling inactive, calm you down when you are anxious, and so on. Music can also feed your soul and help to heal you. Have you ever noticed that when you are angry you may play really loud music? This is because music helps you to express to the world how you are feeling. Music also has destructive uses, like playing your music loud when your lover's trying to catch up on some sleep, or playing music which others dislike to deliberately wind them up. However, playing music which you and others feel comfortable with can help to enhance your lives with positivity.

94/4

Find Humility

Being humble doesn't mean that you go around with your head drooped, bowing to others all day. Humility is something you find within yourself; a recognition that your personality, wants and desires are in effect humble to the expression of your soul. When you are humble you surrender to life in appreciation of who you are – a divine being – not of what you are, or what you have achieved. Being humble puts you in a position of truth that life is how it is. When you have humility you are able to see life as a gift, which it is, and an opportunity for learning, and for growth. Finding humility is a wonderful quality to help you make the most out of your life.

95/5

Think Before You Speak

Sometimes you may feel mentally exhausted from having talked incessantly. Perhaps talking to the public plays a large role in your life if you work as a teacher, in personnel, and so on. Your mind can get so clogged up with information that you forget what you are saying. Perhaps you are a shop assistant serving two customers at once; one customer wants a green jacket and the other wants a red blouse, and you confuse the two. You may also, without thinking, say to one customer, 'It doesn't flatter you at all.' Learning to think of others, and be discriminating in what you say, may help to bring more clarity into your life.

96/6

Eat Good Foods

Eating good foods is not just a matter of eating what is right for your own body type and your particular constitution, but is also about eating foods that look, smell, taste and feel good to eat too. Indeed your eyes visually enjoy good food before you even have a chance to eat it, and as your eyes are the 'windows of your soul' then your soul is feasting too. You may enjoy eating colourful foods and like them at different times. In cold weather, for example, you may like to eat bright orange or red foods which may warm you up simply by stimulating you with their visual vibration. Good foods may also be ones which are organic, healthy or right for you at any moment in time.

97/7

Learn To Trust

If you are searching for the meaning of life within yourself then the only thing you can ever do is trust. By trusting what you find, and knowing that it is relevant information for you at that time, you are led on to the next moment in your life. For example, you may be pondering upon a specific problem, and by meditating or going inside yourself for a time, a solution to the problem may arise. Learn to trust that life gives you what you need in order for you to learn your lessons, so that you can grow stronger from your experiences and be at one with nature.

98/8

Humiliation

Humiliation is a painful experience for your ego or personality to endure and it is one which can leave long-lasting effects upon your psychological behaviour. It can even deter you from trying certain things again. When people try to humiliate you it is because a part of them feels powerless. However, your soul cannot feel humiliation for it knows that everything and everyone is equal at the soul level. But this powerful emotion, humiliation, is a great leveller; if you refuse to feel humiliated when others try their best to put you down then it may help to teach them that you are both equal. Humiliation is food for the soul in the long run.

99/9

The Sun God

Sun gods were worshipped in ancient times, for they were said to bring good fortune and blessings to a person or culture. The sun shines energy on Earth which sustains all life, and without it you would quickly shrivel and die. Indeed, each cell in your body is like crystallized sunlight held together by the energy it relays. Therefore, the sun god is within all of us. Even during difficult times in our lives when we face the 'dark night of the soul', the light is always there. It is up to you to choose to live 'in the light', and to utilize your inner light in a positive way. God is therefore within everyone and we are all connected as one big part of the sun god.

100/1

Find Courage

When you find yourself in new circumstances, bewildered, with people around whom you no longer recognize, with new faces staring you in the eye, learn to be brave. It is at these times when you may need to find your own feet, your own inner strength, and to take the bull by the horns and just carry on. Take a deep breath and face your future now. Perhaps you may want to avoid facing your new direction by creating detours. However, life moves you forwards no matter how much resistance you place on yourself and how hard you try.

101/2

Human Dynamos

Your body is a little powerhouse, constantly carrying out activities which enable you to function. For example, your heart pumps blood, your nerves communicate to each other, your muscles expand and contract, and so on – you are a human dynamo. This means that even during times when you are lounging around like a lizard in the sun, you are still being dynamic. It may help you to recognize this so that you can consciously tap into all this dynamic energy inside you and utilize it in some way. Perhaps this means picking up a book and reading, doing some exercise or making love – whatever. Energy is there to be used physically, emotionally, mentally and spiritually. Indeed, the inner source (from your soul) is never ending.

102/3

Be Innocent

Within us all, however hard it may sometimes seem, is a childlike innocence, the part of ourselves which is like a child new to life. Some people are very cynical and feel that they have seen it all and done it all before, that there is nothing left that will shock them, or disturb them from their false sense of know-it-all-ness. But even the most hardened cynic can melt like butter when something innocently touches their life. For example, perhaps it is a sentimental scene which moves them, or a delicate flower, or some kindness which is carried out on their behalf. Innocence is refreshing, renewing, and rekindles you with your inner source, your soul. It is innocence which can help you to grow.

103/4

Find Your Boundaries

Boundaries are laid down in all areas of life to keep things flowing. In the office, for example, 'pigeon holes' and 'in-trays' help people to work efficiently. If employees needed to sort through a huge pile of documents to find their correspondence, it would be very time-consuming indeed. As within an office, boundaries in relationships and in life also help things to run more smoothly. But in order for you to set boundaries with others you need to be able to recognize what these boundaries are. For example, if you know that you need 15 minutes alone in your room before dinner then you can proceed to ask others to adhere to this. At the end of the day, boundaries help you to feel safe and therefore function more comfortably in life.

104/5

Be Clear

At times when you are crystal clear about what it is you want or need in your life then you are more likely to attract those very things to you. For example, you may be house-hunting and be very clear that you need spacious rooms, a gorgeous leafy garden, and that you need to find the house by a specific date. Your clarity of mind sends clear thoughts into the universe which gathers energy to help manifest these very needs. Being clear with people in the way you communicate your needs can also help you maintain good relations with them, and enable them to be clear about what they need from you. Moments of clarity can occur at any given time.

105/6

Find Comfort Within

When you feel uncomfortable you may wish that others could do something to make you feel better. For example, you have to give a speech to a large group of people and you are feeling very anxious. Five minutes to go and you just wish somebody else could go on instead. However, it is at these times of great opportunity when you can learn to reach inside to your own reserves to comfort yourself. Perhaps you tell yourself, 'It'll be OK, I can do it', or say to yourself, 'If I make a mistake it doesn't matter because I'm only human, for goodness sake'. You may comfort yourself by breathing deeply or doing some stretch exercises on the spot to release tension. Take responsibility for yourself.

106/7

Be Honest

Honesty is a good feeling because when you are honest you can relax, and it frees up all your energy. If you have, for example, been telling white lies to your sister (even if you think it is to protect her in some way) then you hold this tension within yourself. Lies contribute towards slowing down the free-flowing energy in your whole mind, body and spirit, which are all connected. By 'getting something off your chest' and 'coming clean' about some lie you have been holding on to, energy is released which can lighten your load and lighten you up. At the end of the day, honesty really is the best policy for all concerned.

107/8

Live For Today

When you appreciate life and don't take it for granted, you are more likely to be able to live in the moment and live for today; after all, yesterday has gone and tomorrow is a lifetime away. Making the most of what you are doing right now means that when this moment has gone you can say 'I gave it my best shot' no matter what. Then you can go to sleep knowing that you are at peace with the day. Living for today does not mean that you do not think of what you would like to do in the future because you still have your dreams, ideas and plans. It simply means that the future is just that, and it is now where your attention is needed.

108/9

Life Is An Experiment

The whole of life is like one big experiment and you never know how it is going to turn out. When you are cooking, for example, recipes don't always work even when you have followed them meticulously. Perhaps you have baked bread many times but sometimes it ends up being too sticky, too dry, it doesn't rise, and so on. Nothing's guaranteed. Therefore the best you can do each day is to enjoy experimenting with life. Perhaps you like to try new make-up, new clothes, go to new places, or find resourceful ways to experiment in your daily routine. Knowing life is an experiment can also help to lift the pressure off getting it right, because who can say exactly what the correct recipe is?

109/1

Explore Life

Have you ever explored the contents of old cupboards at home which have not been touched for months, or years? Your eyes simply marvel at the sight. Perhaps you find books you had been looking for but never found, clothes which you had forgotten about but which would brighten up your wardrobe, old love letters which remind you of relationships in the past, and much more. Each day that you go out into the world is also a 'Pandora's box' because you never know just what you'll find, what you'll learn, or what is around the corner and about to come your way. So today be open to life and to all its treasures.

110/2

Wear Something New

Wearing something new – whether it is a whole new out-fit or simply a piece of jewellery – can inspire you with new energy. Clothes carry vibrations from the people who wear them, and wearing new clothes which are empty of any vibes (except for the people who made or designed them) may make you feel like a new person too. Each garment or item you wear says something about you, and wearing different styles of clothing is one way for you to get into contact with different aspects within yourself. For example, you may feel more 'in control' when you wear smart suits, or feel laid back by putting on a pair of jeans. Clothes influence the way you think and feel, and can also influence the way others perceive you.

111/3

Your Guardian Angel

When you have found yourself in difficult situations, or at times when you feel you need to make big decisions about your life, you may like to turn to your spirit guides or guardian angels who are always by your side. These represent inner aspects of yourself and are energies which are available for you to tap into during times of need. These energies carry with them great wisdom, and so do you from lessons you have learned in the past through all your experiences. Your guides communicate with you often as you go about your daily life but you may not always be aware of this. Sometimes you may like to create space in your life to be quiet and to consciously connect with them and with your inner self.

112/4

Share A Hug

Hugging is one way to feel your humanness as you make physical contact with another person, be it a lover, friend, family member or even a complete stranger. Perhaps you hug a friend and they don't hug back because they are too busy enjoying being held. Or perhaps you are the one relishing a bear hug; perhaps you are unable to hug them back because you have big, strong arms hugging you. Hugging is one good way to show you care for others and to learn to share yourself with them too. It's easy, free and available with someone in your vicinity if you both choose. Hugging enables you to let others get close to you on many levels.

113/5

Be Happy

Happiness is an emotion which means that you feel good, and choosing to take a happy outlook can bring even more happiness into your life, because like attracts like. For example, if you are skipping down the road people may see you and think 'Oh, she looks happy' and they may also feel your happiness as it radiates out to them. People may be cheered up simply by looking at your happy smile or by listening to the happy sound of your voice. At home or work others may mirror your happiness by smiling too. Happiness is transitional and not something you can hold on to – feelings change – so learn to make the most out of happiness when it shines your way.

114/6

Learn To Prioritize

Whether you have an endless shopping list of things to do each day or just a few, learning to prioritize things by way of their importance and necessity is very useful. For example, in your day you may need to take your children to school, book some tickets for your business trip, buy some groceries, finish a work project, and all of these things are essential. But putting them into some kind of priority can help you manage your life; perhaps you decide shopping for groceries can actually be done another day so that you can finish your work project, and so on. It is only you who can decide what your priorities are, and you make your own choices in life.

115/7

Be Inspired By Poetry

Words and poems that connect with soul can move you deeply when you read them, and romantic poems can inspire you with their beauty and love; they may even bring you to tears. Words are very powerful; the feelings and thoughts of the poet bring them alive. Poems are one way of expressing yourself in life. Perhaps you write intimate poetry for yourself and keep it private and hidden away from others' gaze. Or you may write poetry to share your thoughts and feelings of life with others; perhaps you narrate these as little stories to those who choose to listen and be inspired by your poetry.

116/8

Try Breathing

When you are relaxed your breathing happens easily as you inhale and exhale life, but when you are tired, anxious or stressed your breathing may seem laboured, and you sigh. You may not notice that you aren't breathing properly because you are so busy focusing outside yourself, and you may even go for long periods of time like this. Breathing is a natural process but sometimes paying a little attention each day to this mechanism can remind you to relax. Exercise is one very good way to encourage deep breathing, and some meditation techniques can help to regulate your breathing too. However, it is useful to find something that suits you and also to enjoy the things that you do. Today, be aware of your breath.

117/9

A Fast Mover

When you are focused on what you want in your life then you may be able to get things done fast. This is because when you are sure about what you want you may brim over with confidence and go for these things full on. For example, perhaps you want to design and build your own sports car and you don't let the fact that you have no practical experience hamper your efforts or deter you from your goal. Indeed, perhaps you have experts who can advise you what to do and explain things in a step-by-step way; your inner drive leads you the rest of the way. Even if your design proves to be a flop then by concentrating your willpower on your next project, you can progress your life in other areas if you choose.

118/1

Be A Pioneer

We are all pioneers in some way because we all travel through life in our own unique way. As we do we break down more of our own inner forest of trees (our shadow side) which has darkened our path and we clear a way through into the light. Sometimes we may want to take the old path we know, or want others to lead us down their path, instead of pioneering our own. However, even the most seasoned pioneers find themselves in a dead end from time to time and may spend some time pondering on which direction to take next. Pioneering can be fun and stimulate us with new things to think about and to do with our lives.

119/2

Have Faith In Life

Having faith means being able to carry on with your life knowing that you may not consciously know what you are doing, where you are going, or exactly who you are. It means being able to simply carry on, and being able to have faith that life takes you where you are meant to go, and gives you what you need in order for you to grow. Sometimes you may lose faith in life, but that is just you giving up and losing faith in yourself. Therefore believing in yourself, believing that you have the power to carry on somewhere deep inside of you, can really help you to face life.

120/3

Have A Gossip

Some people say that gossiping is childish, stupid, a waste of time or scandalous, but at times having a gossip about the latest stories in the newspapers or television can really help you to loosen up and relax a little during the day. This is particularly so when the gossip is harmless and humorous, or stories which you can really identify with. Indeed, five minutes of gossip may even help to snap you out of a depression for a while when it's done in a light-hearted way, and may give you something to think about for the rest of the day. Gossip and a cup of tea go together really well, too.

121/4

Enjoy A Walk

Walking can be a gentle or vigorous exercise, which can help you to stay healthy, but it can also nourish and feed your soul. Walking, particularly in open green spaces like gardens, parks and woods, enables you to connect with your inner self, as you breathe in the beauty and joy of nature. Sometimes going for a walk is one good way to help you sort out some problem because it gives you time to think, whilst at the same time it helps to release tension in your body associated with that problem. Walking is a wonderful relaxing pastime to do with your family, lover or with a group of friends, and a gentle stroll after dinner can be a wonderful nightcap.

122/5

Have A Good Cry

You may cry for many reasons: in response to tension or physical pain which has built up in your body; to express sadness or joy; and even to get attention from others. Indeed, crying can be a really productive and useful tool if it helps you to release trauma, for example. At times, having a good cry can help you go through the darkness you may be feeling emotionally, and if you go through it completely, you may then come out into the sunshine at the other end. Crying is frowned upon by some people, but they may be the very people who would benefit from allowing themselves to let go and cry.

123/6

Asking For Your Needs

It is only you who knows what your needs are; others can only guess. Sometimes you may complain that others do not meet your needs, and this may be so. However, perhaps this is because you have not communicated them clearly enough, or perhaps you are confused about whether you actually want some need to be met. Usually life gives you what you need anyway, although this may not be what you think you need, or indeed may not be what you want. When needs are exchanged clearly then life is more likely to flow in all kinds of situations – between colleagues, lovers, friends, and between parents and children.

124/7

Invite Life In

The more you are able to invite life in – like being hospitable to a guest who has travelled a long way – the more of life you can experience and therefore the wiser you can grow. Of course, you can choose to discriminate to some extent about whom you let in and when. For example, only opening your front door to people whom you like, and not to every stranger that comes your way. But some people believe that if someone or something has come their way it is for a reason, and is there to teach them some sort of lesson. Be aware of how far you allow yourself to open your door, and your heart, to life, and to the situations and people which present themselves to you.

125/8

Communicate Powerfully

When you communicate from your inner self, and from a position of truth (your truth), then it means the messages you communicate can be very powerful indeed. For example, you may really need a pay rise because you have extra financial commitments to meet at home. When you communicate this true need to your boss he or she may be more likely to respond to your need positively because they know you are speaking the truth. Imagine another scenario: a fellow colleague asks their boss for more money because you have had a rise and they are jealous; the boss may this time refuse because he or she does not feel their communication to ring true. Today, be aware of how you communicate with others and why.

126/9

Forgiveness Is A Group Need

When you forgive somebody you subconsciously release a whole group of people at once, which allows for much healing. This is because we are all made up of energy, and when an energy block is healed it releases energy from others. For example, you are jealous of your sister having more friends than you. Your partner and your parents particularly get to hear about it. One day you realize that you are happy being you. At this point all of those around you can feel this energetically, and it releases something in them too. The whole world is spiritually and energetically connected, and each time something is healed within you it can influence the whole world in a positive way.

127/1

Your Future Is Now

Every time you think of something you would like to happen in the future, in any area of your life, then by bringing back your attention and your energy to the present moment you can begin to manifest it right now. For example, if you wish to find yourself in a fantastic new job where you can utilize your creative talents, then buying career guides, registering with agencies and going for job interviews can bring you one step towards manifesting your ideal. Of course, sometimes fate plays a hand and guides you in the best possible direction which may not be the one you planned. Today, be aware that everything you say and do is contributing towards your future.

128/2

Great Expectations

Having expectations can at the very least be a clue as to things you would like to do or to have in your life, but by placing any great expectations on life then you may be setting yourself up for failure. For example, you expect to receive an enormous bonus from your boss at the end of the year because you feel you have given your job 150 per cent, but your bonus cheque is only a fraction of what you expected. If you had no previous expectations then you may have been delighted, but as it is it spoils your whole week. However, positive thoughts create positive actions, which can attract positive things to you, and having a positive outlook on life may prove to deliver things which are higher than any of your expectations.

129/3

Be Enthused By Life

Enthusiasm can brighten up your whole life as your inner happiness radiates out to those around you. Perhaps, for example, cooking a lovely meal for you and your family also puts you in a good mood to face those essential chores that need carrying out, or gives you the energy to face difficult situations in your life. If you are enthusiastic about cooking, it may inspire others to experiment with their recipes or even to take a cookery course. Enthusiasm shows you that you are alive and are actively taking an interest in life. Notice those things which fill you with enthusiasm, and things which therefore help to drive you on with your life.

130/4

Roots Anchor You

At times when your life seems shaky right down to your very foundations, learn to let your roots support you and keep you anchored, knowing that whichever way the wind blows you can survive. Roots can be a lot of things. Your roots can be your daily routine which gets you through no matter what. Your roots can also be your connection to your spirituality, to a religion, to a faith, to your inner self, which can help to keep you strong. Indeed, when you go through times of crisis it may seem like it is the people around you who keep you anchored. However, they may contribute enormously, but it is ultimately your own strength which gets you through at the end of the day.

131/5

Follow The Light

It is your inner light which guides you; that part of yourself which is illuminated by your soul, which knows where your journey lies, and tries to direct you upon the best possible path. Sometimes you may think that a book reveals the light to you, or that a person becomes the light of your life, but these things are merely connecting you with your own inner light. Like attracts like. Ultimately we are all connected and therefore a part of the one light, or the one eternal light, and at times when you feel lost, literally lighting a candle (and securing it in a safe place) can help to remind you of this everlasting light.

132/6

Connections

Sometimes, when life is complicated, your attention is drawn to the many different people linked to you or circumstances intertwined with your own. Indeed, even if you did think that you functioned completely separately to anyone else, then stopping to think just how many connections weave their way through your life at any given time may be all that it takes to convince you otherwise. For example, have you ever taken an action and afterwards realized just what an impact it has had on the lives of those around you, that even people you hardly know have been implicated too? It may help you to be aware of any new connections you make and of the existing ones you have too.

133/7

The Bigger Picture

Everyone is human and at times you may get carried away with your own life and forget that there is a big, wide world out there which is all a part of the bigger picture and the bigger plan. Indeed, it is at these very times when you are solely preoccupied with yourself that you are most likely to get 'stuck' with things going around and around in your head or 'stuck' with feelings which seem to blot out any other life out there. At these exact times it may help you to switch on the television and watch the evening news – a reminder of the bigger world in which you live – or to simply open up to listen to how others' lives are going. Everyone is unique and contributes to the bigger picture; this is the beauty of life.

134/8

Don't Try – Do It!

Have you ever wanted something so much that you tried too hard, straining yourself in the process? For example, you really want to make a good impression on a first date. You leave plenty of time to get ready; you make sure you have a scintillating outfit which makes you feel and look good; you sort out all the fine details; but you try so hard that an hour before your date you are completely exhausted. Indeed, you are too tired to focus on the main thing – your date – when he or she arrives. Trying can be very tiring indeed. Learn to be aware of how much energy you put into effort and planning, and leave enough energy for living in the present moment.

135/9

Acceptance

Whether you are experiencing an overall change in your life – in your career, your relationship, your health – or at times when you feel the effects of external changes from others around you, then learning to apply a little acceptance may help. For example, your boss has said that he or she is going to make you redundant due to financial losses. You may fight this by asking your boss to retain you, or give yourself a hard time and blame yourself for doing something wrong, and so on. However, by accepting your boss's decision you can then take appropriate actions to find another job, without losing more unproductive energy over something you can do nothing about. Accepting life is one sure way to allow more of life to flow your way.

136/1

Share Your Purpose

You may feel a very strong sense of purpose in your life; you may know what it is that you are meant to be doing and follow your path with great intent and joy. Perhaps you are an architect who is designing a community centre for a specific area. Sharing your sense of purpose with others can, however, help to improve upon your designs. Perhaps you meet up with residents and share your purpose so that you can create the best possible building for all concerned. When you join together with others with one sole purpose in mind then your energies are intensified, which can create even more powerful results.

137/2

Spring-Cleaning

When winter is over, just as you turn the corner into spring, you may get the urge to spring-clean your home. Perhaps you throw away any old magazines, and bits and pieces which have been hanging around collecting dust, have a good sort through your clothes, and so on. Perhaps you rearrange furniture to bring some new life into your home too. Spring-cleaning gets rid of all the old cobwebs, and like a breath of fresh air breathes new life into you because your outer environment mirrors back aspects of you. Indeed, spring-cleaning needn't be a chore; you can delight in knowing that it is a healing process, as well as revitalizing your environment.

138/3

Confidence

Confidence means that you feel comfortable within yourself, enough that you feel safe to go into the big world and be yourself. People who are confident are usually the first to admit that they make mistakes, but they can live with themselves because they accept this as a normal part of life. For example, you may bubble with confidence as you dance solo in front of an enormous audience for the first time. 'I'll give it a go' you think. You make a few mistakes with the leg work but apart from that you give a sparkling performance and you are satisfied. People comment on the success of your routine, and do not even bother about the small mistakes you made. Confidence gives you the energy to delve into the unknown and to know that, whatever comes your way, you can survive.

139/4

Letting Go

Learning to recognize when it is time to let go of people or things which are no longer needed can help your life to flow. Sometimes, for example, letting go of a relationship which is no longer serving you can make room for new relationships to come into your life, and can inject more energy into your other relationships. Indeed, you can choose how you let go; you can simply accept a situation and make life easier for yourself by just letting go. Or you may feel like you are being forced to let go and therefore make a fuss, kick or scream as you resist the process. Ultimately, your life moves forwards anyway, but participating in this process in a positive way can really help you in the long run.

140/5

Free Up Restrictions

Restrictions can be very helpful. At times when areas of your life are getting out of hand, for example, restricting yourself where appropriate can help you to bring things back into balance. Sometimes you may find the opposite occurs, that you restrict yourself so much that there is not much space left for movement in your life. Perhaps you restrict yourself by having two good friends when you could have more, or you may restrict yourself to one kind of exercise when there are other alternatives for you to choose from, and so on. Try to allow enough movement and restriction to help balance your life.

141/6

Shake Up

Life doesn't generally travel in one straight line, and if it does then not usually for very long. Each day brings something new to inspire you and teach you. When your life runs smoothly then, yes, you are learning, but it is actually during challenging times that you learn the most. Perhaps you have been given a promotion at work and you need to spend more time there and less time with your family and friends. This may turn your life upside down but you can learn through the experience. Shake-ups can enhance your life because they get rid of 'dead wood'. When all the pieces land, they do so exactly as they are meant to be, leaving you to adapt to new things in your life.

142/7

Find Your Identity

When you identify with a quality in someone it is because that element is contained within your make-up already, even though this may be a hidden aspect of which you are not consciously aware. As humans we all identify with each other in some way by the fact that we all have the same basic needs in life, and similar desires too. However, we are also completely unique, and that is what gives us our own identity. For example, nobody plays the piano in quite the same way that you do, or dresses with your own individual style. Finding out who you are and developing your identity can be fun and one of life's great adventures.

143/8

Responsibility

Everyone is capable of being both responsible and irresponsible. Even if you think you are the most responsible citizen on this planet, be aware of those slippery situations which may evade you. For example, you may set a shining example to your work colleagues and never let them down; you can be counted upon to be responsible at all times. But at home you may neglect taking your dog out for a walk, even when you have the time, which highlights a little irresponsibility. Today, be aware of situations that arise which test your sense of responsibility, and be aware of the actions you take and their consequences, both for yourself and for others.

144/9

Forgiveness

When you forgive yourself for something which you feel you have done 'wrong', then you allow for more love and light to come into your life. Indeed, your soul can teach you that there is no right and wrong, and that all the lessons which life teaches you are simply ways of bringing you more into alignment with your true self. When you forgive others you also allow for spirit to touch you with a true sense of reality. Forgiveness means a cancelling out, a letting go of those ways in which you may hold yourself back from living in the light, so that you can function in your place of inner truth. In order to 'for-give' others you always need to give, and to forgive yourself too.

145/1

The Big Adventure

You may think that adventure means climbing along hill tops, skiing down a mountain or racing a horse along a beach, and so on. However, perhaps you can stop for a minute and realize that it is the gift of life itself which is the biggest adventure. Indeed, whatever you do, and even if you do nothing, you are a part of that living adventure every single moment of the day. Like all adventures, you can choose to go for the biggest thrills, or for the smallest risks that are just enough to get your toes wet. Adventures come in all sizes, shapes and form.

146/2

Vitality Is Seductive

When you are brimming over with energy, sparkling and shining bright, then this radiates out to all those around you and lightens up their life. You become seductive. Sometimes you may be unaware of the amount of energy you generate and just how magnetic you are. At other times you may consciously choose to use your radiance to draw others into your life. For example, a potential lover may be mesmerized by your beaming eyes and surrender under the influence of a single glance. Perhaps your vitality for life inspires others to get up and do things with their lives too. Vitality is your life force, your pulse which is set in time with the universal clock.

147/3

Mysticism

If you find yourself reading books about the great mysteries of the universe and life, then the greatest understanding of all is to realize that most of these mysteries contain the simple truths about life. Mysticism is simply another way of looking at life, usually from the soul's perspective instead of viewing life from your earthly body alone. Mysticism is generated from within, information which pours through from your soul and which can help you to feel spiritually connected to people and to the world in which you live. Indeed, it may be said that much mysticism is completely ordinary, and that the most peculiar thing is the outer mysteries of life – the everyday situations which we find ourselves in!

148/4

Learn To Delegate

It is important for everyone to learn to take responsibility for themselves but it is quite another matter to become overburdened by your obligations. For example, perhaps you agree to be a committee leader for a local community project, take on a new role with more authority at work, have another child, take on a larger mortgage, and so on. At these times, learning to delegate duties where you can may help you to expand and move on with your life, and when you delegate to others you are also empowering them with responsibility. Delegating helps to keep things moving in life and frees up some of your time too.

149/5

Living On The Edge

You are born with the capability to experience great
extremes in your life: love and fear, warmth and cold,
prosperity and poverty, and so on. Indeed, it is only by
having some awareness of these qualities over many lifetimes that you can appreciate them fully. For example,
perhaps in the past you were very wealthy materially but
lived in a big house which was very cold, and now you
really appreciate your central heating, or all the wonderful
people around you whose love keeps you warm. In order
to find your centre point you may need to feel what it is
like to live life on the edge for a while, so that you can recognize both aspects and learn to find equilibrium.

150/6

Flirting Is Contagious

When somebody flirts with you it gives you the opportunity to respond or not, and to flirt back if you choose. Flirting is something which you may do innocently and you may be surprised with the attentions that come your way. It is also something which you may do deliberately to 'wind somebody up', in which case be aware that you may have to take responsibility for your actions because karma ensures you get back your just desserts. Flirting is, however, one way of not being direct and expressing openly what you would like to say or do, and the more you flirt the less direct others' response may be too.

151/7

Feel Your Feelings

On 'good days' when everything is going well, you may love feeling your feelings because you feel good. At other times, though, you may not enjoy the feelings you have. Perhaps you have an overwhelming feeling of sadness, and this does not feel comfortable. However, feelings are what make you human and what make you feel alive. Feelings are also one way to relate to people and to share the experience of being human together. Perhaps at times you detach yourself from your feelings, or act in one way when you are feeling something else. You pretend to be happy which masks an underlying feeling of anger or sadness. Feelings are a powerful energy which you can utilize in a positive way to teach you more about life.

152/8

Drunk On Life

There must be some elements of life which you enjoy because your animal instincts keep you coming back for more, as you are reborn time and time again. Indeed, life is like a drug which you can't get enough of in relation to your ego, but your soul knows what you need in the long run. Unlike drugs, chocolate, food, alcohol, and so on, life is free, and you don't need to pay an entry or exit fee. Your drugs are earth, air, fire and water – that's all you need. Sometimes your senses are acute, and you experience things deeply, whilst at other times life seems a blur as clarity fails you. 'Why am I here? Who am I?' you mumble to yourself in despair. Dying is like coming off a drug, but eventually you can learn to let go of this drug and to be free.

153/9

Addictions

For some people, addictions are ways of getting into life or they may help them survive difficult situations. For example, perhaps you are going through a divorce and you become addicted to watching television in the evenings, which is uncharacteristic of you as it has hardly magnetized you before. Some addictions can be dangerous to your health, of course, but it is your choice whether to keep them or give them up. Perhaps you can look upon addictions as a purification process which is cleansing and unleashing parts of you which need to be expressed and healed. Letting go of addictions eventually helps to bring you into deeper levels of wholeness.

154/1

Gardening

Whether you have a huge garden to play around with or simply decorative window boxes or potted plants, you can still enjoy gardening. Perhaps you are stimulated by being outdoors in fresh air and natural daylight, or you enjoy getting all muddy or sandy from pottering around in the earth. Perhaps you enjoy the design, or nurturing aspects of gardening too. Earth is one element that supports life; when you die your ashes return to the earth. In your garden you can observe the natural cycles of life and death in the seasons. Each time you sow some seeds it is a new beginning; you can watch them grow into plants which eventually wither and die. When you enjoy gardening you are nourishing the earth, yourself and your soul.

155/2

Nature Spirits

Today, be aware of the whole world – both the seen and the unseen. Indeed air, although you cannot see it move, is brimming with energy and life. Human energy vibrates very slowly compared to other dimensions around us. For example, fairies, elves, angels, and so on, vibrate at a very fast speed, and sometimes if you are very quick, and open up your inner vision, you can see these energies. Of course, these nature spirits may not look the way you expect them to in dense human forms, but they may appear as shimmers of sparkling energy (like looking at raindrops in the sunshine, only many times brighter). Today, allow yourself to look and see beyond form, beyond your dreams; they are a part of reality. Perhaps it is we who are asleep!

156/3

Like Yourself

Being kind to yourself, and learning to like yourself (as opposed to loving yourself which is very different), on days when situations in life are trying to tell you 'you're not a nice or good person' can be a positive attitude to take. Of course, it may be much easier to like yourself on good days when the sun is shining around you. When you are kind to yourself it allows room for others to be kind to you too because it welcomes them in. Perhaps you can be kind in your attitude towards people around you as well. It may help to focus on the positive aspects that you like about yourself and others, and bring more warmth into the world.

157/4

Breakfast

They say breakfast is the most important meal of the day because it stokes up your energy and gets you moving on your way. So how do you start your day? Do you gulp down any old drink and grab whatever food you see to take with you as you walk down the street? Perhaps you opt out of breakfast altogether? Or do you lounge around enjoying every mouthful with the daily newspaper, or perhaps sit formally with your lover, family or friends? Each day is a new beginning and breakfast is your first meal of the day (no matter what time you eat). So celebrate a brand new day by making the most of breakfast time.

158/5

The Big Sleep

Shut your eyes – where do you go as you slip off into the world of dreams? Why, to connect with your spirit and to nurture your soul in the world of the great unknown. The big sleep is time for inner reflection – sleep is the most natural form of meditation which quietens your mind so that you can get some rest. Of course, sometimes your head works like a computer when you sleep, sorting out problems, with a list of things on its mind. When you sleep you receive inner messages from your subconscious mind. At times you may wake up exhausted – your spirit has done a hard night's work! Sleep is a wonderful time for repair work for your mind, body and spirit. Make time for sleep.

159/6

Family Favourites

Were you a family favourite? As a child, did you receive more love, attention, rewards, and so on, than your siblings? Perhaps you were the 'apple' of your mother or father's eye, or green with envy because you weren't. In this world, however, there is room for everyone. For example, if you cast your thoughts back to your childhood and look around, perhaps you can see that you were highly favoured over others by your aunt, grandparents, or by your nanny. Indeed, there is enough love in the world for everyone, and it is all shared out, by different people and at different times; everyone fits in perfectly somewhere.

160/7

Take A Break

When you have been working or playing very hard then it may help you to take time off for a break. A break may mean travelling to another part of the country or to far-off lands. If you live in a big city you may like to visit the country, but if you live near the sea then a city break may be just the change of scenery you need. A luxury for you may be staying at home and enjoying your own space too. Holidays are useful as they help you to switch off from your regular routine. Sometimes, however, a change can be as good as a rest. For example, changing offices, or moving your desk around to give you a new view at work may enhance your energy and enthusiasm. Perhaps wearing some new item of clothing can help you to feel good and energize you.

161/8

Daydreaming

Everyone has an electro-magnetic field around them, an energy field or aura, and indeed the whole world is made up of atoms of energy. When you daydream a part of your energy body drifts off into another level of consciousness or reality, and you may lose all thoughts of where you are and what you are doing, because your mind is occupied elsewhere. Energy goes where it is needed, and although you are escaping material reality when you daydream, you may be spending essential time elsewhere. Indeed, daydreaming allows your mind to be creative and you can bring back to earth thoughts and ideas which may benefit you. Daydreaming can be very useful, but as the old saying goes, 'there is a time and place for everything'.

162/9

A Bed Of Roses

Life can be a bed of roses because it is your attitude that makes it look rosy or not. Realistically, however, life can't smell sweet and look lovely all the time, but it can help to keep the possibility at the back of your mind. For example, roses come in many colours, not just reds and pinks, and sometimes when life delivers a gift on your 'doorstep' you do not recognize it as a gift of love, and a gift of life. Perhaps you see only the thorns sticking out of the side and not the beautiful rose petals. In life, you are the only one responsible for creating your own bed of roses, through your eyes only, and it is your choice whether to enjoy them or not.

163/1

Look Around You

When you are wrapped up in your own little world it may help you to stop for a minute and look around you. You may see things you haven't noticed before, even though they have always been there, staring you right between your very eyes. For example, have you ever woken up next to your lover and noticed for the first time that he or she has spots? Of course, you may still love your lover, spots or no spots, but you are simply seeing more of the reality around you. By looking around, you open up to new ways of looking at life, and you may see yourself differently too.

164/2

Sexual Healing

When you feel sexual energy you are feeling the power of universal energy going through you. Sexual energy is your life force, that part of you which says, 'I'm alive'. When sexual energy builds up and is not released through sexual activity or by utilizing these creative energies, then you may feel frustrated and angry. Therefore, releasing sexual energy by making love and through sexual self-satisfaction can help to bring your whole mind, body and spirit into balance. Sexual energy is healing. Sometimes, simply feeling this energy fully also allows it to free up.

165/3

Your Own Lover

Everyone has their own lover; your lover is your soul and your personality who dance side by side your whole life through. Your lover is your inner self who expresses love for you no matter what you do. So you are your own lover, you know what turns you on, what whets your appetite, and what you need in life. As your own lover you can learn to take responsibility for satisfying yourself sexually. Once you know what your inner lover needs then you can ask the partner or lover in your life to satisfy them, if he or she so desires. Your soul has created an earthly body so that your spirit can dance and gyrate with life and express this loving energy out to the world.

166/4

Wash Day

Life is like wash day at home. You are given new clothes (a new physical body) which get dirty and soiled from all the negativity you bring home which has accumulated through ordinary day-to-day living. You put your washing into a machine (or have a bath or shower) and wash everything clean. Water, of course, is a human's greatest necessity in life and is a basic need for survival; water is the gift of life. Water (your emotions) washes everything clean. Soap suds help the process along (your body's chemicals help to keep you in balance). Once washed, you now hang your lovely clean washing up to dry in the air (air oxygenates your cells and brings them back to life). Today, be aware of what your soul is cleansing and allow the grime to simply float away.

167/5

Morning Sunshine

When the bright morning sun shines through the window and illuminates your body it puts the spotlight on you, and any imperfections (which are perfectly perfect) are highlighted too. Similarly, when the light of your soul shines through you it brings to the surface aspects contained within your dark shadow side and highlights these too. Everyone has a shadow side, those parts of yourself which feel separate from who you really are (your soul). But the sun (the light from the soul) is warming; it has the power to melt away fear and negativity if you allow it to. Perhaps you try to block out the morning sun to hide yourself away because you are fearful of what you will see and find. Today, throw open the curtains to life and let your soul light shine through.

168/6

Power Games

Power games may seem amusing to the winner for a time, but if you judge life by being a winner or a loser, then this tag may at some point be 'stuck' on you. But you always lose out by playing power games because it is your ego trying to play god to your soul, and you know who ends up winning, don't you? You. Yes the inner you, your soul. Soul life is the most potent and powerful in the end; and soul has no need for control. Indeed, if you play power games, eventually you end up getting your fingers 'burned' as your ego trips you up and gives you a 'headache' for trying. Power games mean that you are still struggling. If you really want an easy life, then give up the games, be in life.

169/7

Points Of View

Do you throw tantrums or argue until you are almost blue in the face in order to get your own point of view across or get your own way? Or perhaps you try emotional black-mail? If you do, then it may help you to look at life from others' points of view. For example, perhaps your partner wants to take you out on Tuesday evening because he wants to go out with his pals on Monday night, which is when you want him to take you out. By flipping over to his point of view, you may be able to find a win-win situation so that you both get your needs met. Sometimes you may feel vulnerable by allowing yourself to see life from the other side, but it can also make for an easier life at times.

170/7

Your Spiritual Connection

Life is spiritual because the whole of life is connected, but sometimes you need little nudges and reminders of this. Perhaps you seek a spiritual connection by meditating in order to reconnect you with your inner self. Or you may go to church to connect through religion, or talk to friends about issues which are deep and meaningful for you, and so on. Being able to see the spiritual connection during times of crisis can also help you. For example, your children are being very rebellious, but by looking past the situation and connecting with your inner self, it can help you to resolve conflicts within you. This may then help to calm down external situations around you as you learn to take on a different approach. You may like to seek inner sanctuary to help you get clarity about your life.

171/9

No Pain No Gain

When you add new exercises to your workout regime, then the next morning you may ache all over. But when you carry on with these exercises, they eventually become integrated into your workout and you may no longer feel any pain. The principle seems to be 'no pain, no gain'. When your soul teaches you lessons they can be very painful for you; perhaps you are learning patience, honesty, or about thoughtfulness. Pain helps you to recognize what work needs to be done, and indeed you can experience pain on one or many levels – physical, emotional, mental or spiritual. Although it may not feel like it at the time, in the long run pain is actually an ally, a friend who lends you a guiding hand. What's your friend teaching you today?

172/1

Spiritual Pain

Pain in a funny sort of way can help you to feel alive – because at least you can feel and you are being human. However, when you feel pain your first reaction may be to shut off: 'Oh I don't want to feel this' is a regular response. But what you are doing is cutting yourself off from a part of yourself and trying to disown this pain and disown a part of you. By simply being open to pain, you can open up to what lessons it may be teaching you. You may think that the biggest pain in this life is physical, emotional or mental pain, but spiritual pain is often the greatest, because at these times you feel separate and cut off from yourself and others. Learn to allow yourself to connect with yourself and others.

173/2

Nature Is Empty

Nature, which includes us, is constantly moving and changing, every single second of the day. When you observe nature it appears full – well it has created humans, animals, minerals, and everything around you. But, actually, nature is an empty vessel which is simply in a state of constant flow. Empty because it contains infinite potential of possibilities, some realized in the here and now and the rest a total mystery yet to unfold. Indeed, you may understand this a little in the way that when you let go of a problem, things start to move, but problems are moving energy in the first place which can simply float away and sort themselves out if you allow them to. Ultimately we are all aligned with the powerful force of nature.

174/3

Look At A Painting

Imagine everything you saw around you was a painting, then can you imagine just how many canvases it would take to paint every frame you saw in one hour, let alone one day? If you were to stop and to observe every detail of those 'paintings', imagine how much information you would gain about life. On a subconscious level, however, your brain is constantly drinking in information from your environment and stacking up the 'paintings' in your mind; you are wise. Colours which you see in the 'paintings' also play a part in influencing your life, along with the sounds you hear. Today, be aware of all the 'paintings' around you, and also of any paintings you own or may see in art galleries.

175/4

Food For The Soul

Your body loves to be fed on food; your emotions need feeding by expressing your feelings and sharing them with others; and your mind actively needs to be fed with knowledge and information. Your whole mind, body and spirit are all fed on love. However, a good way to feed your soul is for you to do the personal development work that you need to do. Your soul loves this because you are learning the lessons which you need, and therefore growing in spirit and strengthening yourself. Feeding your soul doesn't mean that you need to be good all the time but simply that you live and learn by your mistakes and then move on. Today, learn to feed your earthly being and your soul.

176/5

Lovely Butterflies

Humans are like little butterflies who flit from one flower to another, braving the weather with their delicate little wings, and then being reborn as a caterpillar in their next lifetime (the caterpillar is their childhood phase!). Humans flit from one lifetime to another enjoying the good life (being fed on nice things to eat, with beauty all around), weathering hardship and poverty (ignorance), whilst growing in spirit as we learn and then move on. Like a butterfly, perhaps you settle in one lovely spot in the sunshine for a long time, but you may travel restlessly through the forest at times, hardly catching your breath in order simply to survive during others. Life is delicate but your soul is strong.

177/6

Fantasy Island

Do you live on fantasy island, tucked away all neat and secure in your mind where nobody can reach you apart from other islanders who join in your fantasy? Fantasies are wonderful because they can give you clues as to things you may like to materialize for yourself in life. But many fantasies remain just that, something out of human reach. For example, perhaps you fantasize about winning the World Chess Championship, but if you can't even play chess then now may be the time to begin. Fantasies are thoughts within your mind, but energy follows where your thoughts go, so be aware that what you think and dream may even come true.

178/7

A Quest

Life is like a quest to find the Holy Grail, a searching for what you are looking for – the way home. Home is, of course, your soul which guides you through your life. You may have many earthly quests. For example, a quest to be liked, a quest to be the best, a quest to be a good leader, or a quest to make pots of money, and so on. But each quest you make is there to help you learn the lessons your soul is teaching you in life; and the quests you find yourself on are synchronistic to exactly what it is you need to learn. Today, be aware of the quests in your life; it does not matter if you do not complete all of them because there is more that can be done later on.

179/8

Culture

Cultures are what give flavour to the food of life; imagine if everyone looked the same, followed the same routine, shared exactly the same outlook – how uninteresting life would be! Cultures enrich the world like different soils which nourish people. You may have been born in England, for example, and therefore are influenced by the English culture, but you may also identify with the German, or with the Indian culture, and so on. Perhaps this makes itself noticeable in your life by the way you dress, the foods you eat, the way you speak, or by some of your interests. Everyone can learn from everyone else and ultimately mankind is one soul, one race, learning and sharing together on one planet – Earth.

180/9

Law And Order

There are earthly laws which govern you and which are dictated by politicians and leaders in the country where you reside; each country makes laws according to its own particular outlook on life to serve the people on that land. There are also the laws of nature – spiritual laws which govern you according to your karma (or what you have done in the past), and the karma of that nation and that particular land. You are a spiritual being living in the material plane, and therefore you are being asked to live in alignment with both of these laws. Laws are there to serve you, to guide you through life; a law is there to help teach you about responsibility and help you learn the lessons you need to learn in your lifetime.

181/1

Take A New Step Forwards

Each time you take a new step forwards your whole energy goes with you and makes that step a very powerful move indeed. For example, you may decide to change career, and making that decision is your first step towards making your new career a real possibility. Each step you take brings you nearer to your goal, but of course there may be many, many steps in between, and each one is as important as the next. Everything that happens to you in life starts out from one step into the big unknown; who knows where you will end up or who you will eventually become? Today, be aware of each new step you take.

182/2

Sensitivity Is A Gift

Sometimes when you feel very emotional it may be because you have been over-sensitive to people or to the world in which you live. Perhaps you also feel too open and vulnerable at times and do not enjoy the feeling very much. However, it is this incredible sensitivity you may have to your environment which allows you to let in life, and therefore your sensitivity is in effect a great gift. Perhaps you can find ways of utilizing this quality in order to serve yourself and others. For example, if you are a counsellor then you can use your sensitivity to feel people's pain and suffering, which may in turn help you to help them with the support you give. Sensitivity to your soul is also a positive quality to possess.

183/3

Are You Stubborn?

You can be stubborn in different ways. You may be stubborn because you feel you need to do something that your soul is asking you to do, like setting up a healing centre for example, and you do not give way, even when your family or friends try to persuade you it is not the right thing for you to do. You can also be stubborn because your ego or personality wants something selfishly, and you stamp your feet and demand you get it (pride sometimes comes before a fall). Being stubborn can teach you about what you value, what you need, and about what you don't need, too. However, it is helpful to recognize when your need is a true one and is worth standing up for; and at these times you may find you get your needs met effortlessly.

184/4

Temptation

Everyone is prone to temptation. In life, you may enjoy being tempted to try new things. For example, perhaps your sister makes a wonderful chocolate cream cake and tempts you with it over the telephone, so you rush over to her home. Perhaps you tempt your partner sexually by wearing an attractive outfit on a dinner date which he or she can't wait to explore. Sometimes you may also use temptation to manipulate people. Perhaps your boss tempts you with a raise in salary if you work overtime on a project, even though they have no intention of following this through. Learn to be aware of the tempter and the temptress within you.

185/5

You Are A Messenger

Everyone has the responsibility of delivering messages to the world. It may simply be that you give messages to those around you, or you may be responsible for delivering messages to a whole community. The most powerful messages come from your inner knowledge and truth, and when you communicate them to others, you may be a very powerful teacher for them, and for you too as they mirror back these messages to you. For example, perhaps you give the message to your boyfriend that you are not ready for a long-term commitment, and this may be mirrored back in his behaviour, and so on. When you know what messages you wish to give then this can help everyone concerned.

186/6

Owning Ourselves

Whatever material possessions you own in your life – whether these be masses or very few – at the end of the day you own your body and are connected to that spirituality deep inside which sustains you. Sometimes you may feel disconnected and that you can't relate to life, or you may feel unable to get a grip on things. Perhaps this is because you see the material world as somewhere unsafe or because you simply do not want to connect to life on the material plane at times. However, as you go through life you may learn little by little to own all the parts of you and to call them back in. You can face each fear with love and compassion so that you can feel safer in the world.

187/7

Telepathy

Telepathy is a very easy and potent way of communicating; like writing a letter, you simply compose in your mind the message that you need to say, and then send the message to the person at the other end by thought form: 'this message is for you, thank you'. They say dolphins are very magnetic and are sensitive to these fine thoughts or energy waves, but as humans we are too. Perhaps you find telepathy easy and you consciously give and receive messages freely, or perhaps you can practise with somebody close to you, and work on this muscle if you choose. People may also communicate by exchanging these messages at times when both parties are not consciously aware. Notice how effective telepathy can be at times.

188/8

Be Mobile

When you find yourself locked in situations which just aren't moving, then it may help you to remain mobile. For example, perhaps you are buying a property and have been waiting ages for the other party to complete their own sale before they can buy your home, and this temporarily holds you up from moving on. In life, however, things generally happen for a good reason, and situations move forwards the way they are meant to, which is not always the way in which you would want. This may mean the sale falls through and you end up buying another property which turns out to be for the best. Being mobile doesn't mean giving up what you want, but simply allows you to be flexible to life for your own highest good.

189/9

Ask For Help

Times when you are being a 'know it all' are usually times when you can easily get lost, find yourself off course, and indeed end up not knowing where you are going at all. For example, you give a lecture about pollution – you really think you are the world's expert. But some members of the public question you and reveal from their knowledge that you do not 'know it all' after all. However, the best thing a 'know it all' can do is learn how to ask for help, how to ask questions from people and ask questions of life; this way everyone gets to learn more about life. The potential of your soul to teach you about life is endless; therefore you may realize that it is only your ego that thinks it 'knows it all', at all, at all…

190/1

Wipe Out

Each time you learn important lessons, what you are sub-consciously doing is wiping out things from the past and letting them go. For example, if you learn to allow a member of your family to use the bathroom before you in the morning, then you are relinquishing your need to be self-ish. When you behave like this you release much energy associated with this trait from all the times you have been selfish in the past. Wiping out the past in some way can only happen when you have truly learned the lessons that those situations in life were teaching you. Wiping out the past helps pave the way for new things for you to learn, new directions to follow if you choose, and can help to create openings to allow new people to enter your life too.

191/2

Be Reasonable

When you stamp your feet and demand things of yourself and others, you are making life more difficult for yourself, because you are not being reasonable. For example, you may demand that your lover finishes work at exactly 5pm in order to take you out on a date, even though he or she is very busy. Being reasonable means that you are able to see the bigger picture and to do what's best for both of you. It also means applying logic to a situation, which may over-ride any emotions you may be feeling at the time. So in the above scenario, being reasonable means that you may shift your date to 6.30pm for your lover's convenience, and also for yours, because you realize that you can make good use of the extra time too. Life has time for everybody.

192/3

Express Your Inner Knowledge

Inner knowledge is accumulated from your experience over many lifetimes, and each minute you are adding to this file, whilst at the same time understanding more about lessons you have learned in the past. Therefore, everyone has knowledge to share with others in some way. You may, for example, be knowledgeable about how to care for animals, and the more you carry out these tasks the more you can draw upon your knowledge from the past to help you. Today, be aware that you are constantly passing on your inner knowledge to others. Perhaps you may like to make a mental note of ways in which you do this, or ask your partner, close friends and family to let you know what inner knowledge you share with them, and give them back the compliments too.

193/4

A Recorder Of Wisdom

In our minds is stored information about who we are, where we have come from, and to a certain extent where we may be heading with our lives. There are also collective recordings stored within us which link us subconsciously with humanity, and we can 'read from' these too. However, each generation has recordings of what its era represented, in the form of books, films and art, among others. Indeed, if you visit a library, museum or art gallery and witness what was written at a particular time, you can more fully understand what that particular society was learning about collectively. Life is rich with knowledge but your mind is wealthy too.

194/5

Stop And Start

Life may seem to stop and start. One minute you are zooming forwards and life is whizzing while you are thoroughly enjoying every minute, and at other times it may seem that everything has gone into suspended animation. However, the 'stop' times enable you to catch your breath, to evaluate what you have learned when you were running frantically around, and also give you energy to move fast forwards again. Indeed, even when things seem to be suspended at the physical level, for example, then lots may be happening on the emotional, mental or spiritual planes for you. Life is a constant balancing act, and 'stop' and 'start' times are both essential aspects of this cycle.

195/6

Risk Taking

Cars are considered safe when they are parked and stationary, but that's not what cars are for – they are meant to take you from A to B. Driving can be dangerous, with all the other vehicles on the road darting and dashing about, and every time you go on a journey in your car you are taking a risk. Wearing your seat belt and driving with care can help to minimize that risk; you can take responsibility for yourself. However, you can't take responsibility for others along your path; life is like that. Today, be aware of the risks you take in your life – perhaps potential huge risks, like investing in the stock market, and so on, to little risks, like being friendly to a neighbour with whom you don't normally converse.

196/7

Are You A Pushover?

When you are strong in who you are – you feel comfortable within yourself – then you are able to stand up for yourself and be assertive without needing to control or overpower others when you do so. Power comes from within and it is natural to everyone. Some people may try to use this power to hurt you and to push you around. For example, perhaps your boss expects you to say 'yes' to anything they push your way because they pay you such a good wage. However, being a pushover or a victim does not help you or anyone because nobody wins when energy is abused in this way. When you are connected to your inner spiritual light, everything is equal.

197/8

Forceful

When you try to force things to go your way, nothing or very little tends to happen. Indeed, perhaps the situation you desire may go the other way. In this life everything moves in cycles: the moon and sun cycles, the seasons, day and night, and so on. You mere mortal cannot get the sun to shine longer because you want a tan – nature wouldn't even answer you back, small fry! However, when you can observe natural cycles in your own life then the force – or the energy flow – goes with you at the best possible time. Learn to be aware of how you and others use force to get your own way, observe the consequences, and learn from these situations.

198/9

Superiority Complex

Believing yourself to be superior to others and going around all aloof with your nose stuck up in the air is an illusion, and a funny one at that, because everyone is born of the same essence – we are all spiritually connected and are therefore equal. Having a superiority complex means, however, that you are feeling separate, and unfortunately it is you who is suffering more than those you choose to intimidate with false ideas of grandeur. Indeed, superiority often masks deep feelings of inadequacy, and this may filter out into all areas of your life. Learning to laugh at yourself (in an affectionate way) at times when you find yourself taking this superior stance may help you to connect with others and is one step towards releasing this pattern.

199/1

Give Yourself Permission

Each decision, no matter how small, is important because the actions you take form the basis for further decisions and actions later on. At these times you may ask others for their good advice and want them to tell you what to do. You may even ask for their permission to make a decision about what you 'should' do. For example, you may want your father's permission to marry your boyfriend. Although this tradition is outdated in Western culture, you may choose not to get married without a 'yes' from him as it may be important to you. Cultural rituals like these can be respected, but ultimately you can give yourself permission to do the things which you need to do with your life; you are responsible for what you do.

200/2

A World In Need

We are all needy people; that is, we have needs. For example, you are going through a divorce and you find that you need more emotional support from your friends and family than you would normally. Perhaps you ring them all the time, and they understand and ring you too. However, emotional neediness can also be used as a way of avoiding facing up to your feelings. Perhaps, for example, you have problems within your marriage (like many other people), and you talk about it incessantly and demand others' time. They may not want to talk about your problems because they feel you are neglecting to deal with your own emotions or situation. Others can help to meet your needs when you share with them and when they choose, but you are primarily responsible for meeting your own needs.

201/3

Good News

Good news is contagious. That is, have you ever noticed that when you receive good news you may run to share it with others quickly, particularly with those nearest and dearest to you, and this brightens their lives for a moment too? For example, perhaps you tell your parents that you are expecting your first child. They in turn pass the good news on to extended family, and indeed to anyone who will listen; good news travels fast. Can you imagine how many people are touched with your good news and how much positive energy you may bring into others' lives, even if it's simply for a few moments? Learn to share some good news with others. It doesn't matter how trivial or important it may seem to you; your good news will inject more positivity into the world around you.

202/4

I Hurt

It is the little 'I', the ego, that hurts, at times when it is feeling shut off from its inner source of light – spirituality. Sometimes when you hurt and feel pain you may say to those around you, 'Don't touch me or come too close'. This keeps you in a splendid state of isolation for a while. Life is constantly changing, however, and sooner or later nature moves you on; you feel the light rushing in again and you feel safe. Indeed, times of pain and hurt are times of growth which can encourage you to do some soul-searching. It may help you to realize that at any time at least one part of nature is screaming out for help; so learn to listen.

203/5

A Little Romance

Even if you are the most practical and down-to-earth person, you may still benefit from a little flurry of romance in your life. Your partner, for instance, may wake you up by gently nibbling your ear whilst whispering sweet nothings, or buy you a special box of chocolates for no specific reason. Romance gets you in contact with your feelings; it opens your heart a little wider, and what a wonderful way to experience any day. Indeed, being open to love means that you are also open to life, and with sunshine surrounding you as you go about your daily routine, you may be able to accomplish even more.

204/6

Wine Taster

Do you have a fine ear or fine taste? Perhaps you like listening to classical music and can single out each and every instrument, or you may like to surround yourself with the finest clothes, furniture, and all the fine things there are to buy in life. You may also have a taste for fine wines. A professional wine taster knows that you need all your senses to do a good job. For example, you observe the colour of the wine, you smell its bouquet, you hear the sounds as you whirl it around the glass … and then you taste it and feel it in the pit of your stomach. It touches you. The wine taster has learned how to bring the whole of life into this simple process; today, be aware of all the aspects contained within life.

205/7

Documentaries

Life is like making a documentary. We are all doing
endless research into the topic (life) until we come up
with the answer (the programme) – only to find that later
on somebody else makes another documentary on the
same subject which gives an even deeper view, or even
a completely different view. Making a documentary
requires a lot of people who share the same vision, and a
constant pulling together of resources in order to make it
happen. Today, be aware of ways in which you are working with others and creating your own group vision of the
world. Also, be willing to change your vision to adapt to
new information which comes your way.

206/8

Share Your Work

Being able to share with others can help you maintain a happy and more successful life. This is because, when you work towards meeting everyone's needs, then everyone is more likely to feel satisfied at the end of the day. For example, perhaps you have lots of housework to do before your mother-in-law comes to visit for your birthday. Perhaps your son James wants you to help him with his homework but you are too busy. However, James volunteers to share the housework with you, and then you have time to help him with his homework. Success on a plate for both parties. Learning to share helps create equilibrium at home, in the work place and in life.

207/9

All Or Nothing

Some seeds which you sow may materialize into great things; others may fail to germinate; whilst others still are slow movers, and given time and space they may eventually grow. Perhaps you think that the seeds which flourish can teach you the most about life, but the slow movers and the ones that don't germinate can teach you the most profound and meaningful lessons too. For example, you may have tried to create a child for a long time with no success. This may be very painful in many respects, but at the same time the very process may in some way change your life for the better. Indeed, it may make you appreciate what you have already, or make any further success you may have very much worth the wait. Life isn't black and white; the grey areas are the most significant.

226

208/1

Grow Up

Growing up is an interesting time, full of contradictions and confusion, when you learn to form your own identity and develop your own observations and opinions about life. As adults, however, there is always a part within us that remains childlike, and it is called our 'inner child'. This may rear its head when you are confronted by situations from the past; you may compulsively react like a reflex action from banging your knee against something hard. However, at these times we can learn to say to ourselves, 'here we go again' and we can choose to act, rather than react to life. It is challenging to be an adult and act all grown-up all of the time, but the more we do the more we may be able to forge an easier path for ourselves through life.

209/2

A Problem Shared

There is a saying that 'a problem shared is a problem halved'. This may be because, when you share things with others, you can double up on any solutions to be found. Indeed, you only serve to make your life more difficult by turning problems over in your mind, time and time again, with your thoughts going nowhere. When you talk over your problem, the answer may jump into your mind, and by the end of the conversation there may be no problem at all. Sharing problems also allows others to learn about life and can teach them valuable lessons. Learn to share your problems with others and free up the space to receive help and guidance from them and from your inner self.

210/3

The Life Force

Your inner life force, the energy which drives you forwards, comes steadily flowing through. At times, however, your life force may seem slow and you may feel a little disconnected; at other times it may energize you. Witnessing or experiencing childbirth is one way to see this life force at work. It is the life force of the mother and the child which delivers the baby into the world. Contractions tell the mother when to push and help her baby into the world. They also let her know when to take a rest, to allow the child to gather its resources. The life force ebbs and flows every moment of the day. Being aware of when to expand and when to hold back can help you to make the most out of your life.

211/4

Rejection

Rejection is a feeling which you take on when you feel pushed out or excluded from life. For example, your partner may say that he or she does not like the food you prepared for supper, and you may feel rejected by that, and perhaps you retaliate by being argumentative. However, your partner's comments may not have been aimed at you; perhaps the food simply did not appeal to his or her taste buds at the time, or perhaps it was hot food and your partner wanted something cold, and so on. Everyone has different needs and are entitled to their own experiences, and it may help you to stop taking life so personally. Indeed, between souls, rejection doesn't exist.

212/5

Stay Calm In A Storm

Learning to stay calm at times when life is hectic can help others to stay calm too. Staying calm and centred means that you manage to keep your head above water even when you find yourself in a sinking ship, when the waves are dashing up against you and the winds are cold and bite hard. Staying centred means that you can think your way out of a situation logically, and you may also use your gut instincts to help you. Being calm means that you can weigh up the situation you are in and look at things from both sides, then make decisions which may help to bring harmony for everyone concerned. Staying calm means that you can breathe easily, and breathe away problems naturally when they try to cling to you.

213/6

Emotional Traumas

You may experience traumas in your life which cut you to the bone; the intensity of your feelings may be so great that they become almost unbearable, and you feel like you cannot carry on. However, this may be how you are feeling now, but in another minute, an hour or a day, these painful feelings may fade away. Feelings are powerful but they are changing all the time, and eventually time moves your feelings on. You can also help yourself to feel better by gently using your logical brain to pull yourself out of the depths of despair. Perhaps your mind says 'you need to eat' so you cook yourself a lovely meal, or your mind says 'need some exercise' so you go out for a stroll, and so on. Today, allow feelings to pass through you; tomorrow is another day.

214/7

Make Peace With Yourself

Your soul and your ego are both working together, albeit in different ways, to teach you the lessons you need to learn in life. Sometimes your ego puts up a fight and doesn't want to listen or to do the work it needs to, but eventually breakthrough occurs and life moves on. Making peace with yourself over an issue means that, even for a short while, your soul and ego have given up the fight and are walking together hand in hand. For example, your ego wants dependency but your soul is teaching you to be free, and you find a balance between these two for a while. Today, be aware of how these two aspects of yourself are acting, and encourage them to make friends and even to become playmates and have fun together.

215/8

Cooperation Saves The Day

When you have spent all your energy fighting with your brother over whose turn it is to do the washing up, for example, then you may both fall down into an exhausted heap and neither of you accomplish this task immediately. Your brother thinks that it is always 'his turn' and complains that you never do your fair share; however, this still doesn't get the task done. After due consideration you come up with a solution, and decide that from now on, your brother washes and you dry – you become a team. Learn to find ways of cooperating with those around you, and cooperating with life, because when you do, you can skip through situations and break down barriers which previously appeared impassable.

216/9

Merging Together

Whether as an individual or as a company, merging together with others can help you feel what it is like to be in a partnership, working or living together with others and learning to get along as a collaborative team. Merging doesn't mean that you lose yourself or your identity; it simply means that you forge an additional identity with someone or something else. Merging takes a lot of courage – to be able to allow others to get close to you personally or professionally – but ultimately it may be the best for all concerned. Indeed, when you merge and pool all your resources and ideas and channel them with a specific focus in mind, then great results may be achieved and many lessons can be learned about life.

217/1

Virgin Life

Every day in some way you may feel like a virgin experiencing something new for the first time, but with lots of other new experiences to come your way. However, your soul carries with it much wisdom accumulated from the past. Each virgin day begins and ends, which leads you into another virgin week or month, and so it goes throughout your life. To experience life in innocence as a virgin, with no expectation of what is to come (on the personality level) means that you may be able to allow yourself to fully encompass each moment and make the most out of each brand-new experience that comes your way. Indeed, every moment is new, and living in the moment is what we are learning to do.

218/2

Be A Devil

The Devil is depicted in many ways – with horns, with evil-looking eyes, with fire flowing from its mouth, and so on – but the devil is simply one half of nature, that is the shadow side of life. The shadow contains all the things which are hidden deep inside us, the parts of ourselves that are separate and cut off from the light of our spirituality. The other half of nature is light, and by shining light or love on the shadow side, hidden aspects surface in order to be brought to our awareness, understood and then healed. For example, selfishness can be eventually transformed into selflessness. Some of these qualities and issues may not resolve themselves overnight, and indeed, some shadow aspects may need to be worked on for a whole lifetime.

219/3

Playing With Words

Sometimes people speak to you so fast that you lose their meaning, and all you may be left with is an odd word here and there which you manage to grasp, and your instincts have to do the rest. However, words are fun; you can use them to invoke certain feelings in other people and to express how you feel; you can play with words to make your speech more interesting and diverse; and words can really stimulate your mind. Sexy words can make brilliant foreplay, and words can clearly let you know where you stand within a situation. Learn to be aware of the words you use and the effects they create; simple words are usually the easiest and the most powerful to exchange. You may like to listen to others speak and incorporate some of their words into your communication.

220/4

Give Too Much?

Do you give too much at home, at work, to those nearest and dearest to you, and to life? Giving is a natural state. In this lifetime, perhaps one of your lessons is to learn to flex this muscle until it has limbered up and works happily alongside all the others. Perhaps you relish giving and get so much divine pleasure out of the things you do, or at times you may feel that you have to give, and you may try to manipulate your way out of these situations whenever you can. Perhaps giving is more comfortable for you than receiving on some levels. However, if you think that you do give a lot, you may like to look around and be aware of all the ways people give to you – either physically, emotionally, mentally or spiritually – in a day. Perhaps both the giving and receiving may be a perfect match after all!

221/5

Make The Most Of Your Time

Time waits for no man, woman or child. Today, concentrate on making the most out of the time you have, and the space and time you are in. Time is as precious as the rarest mineral, but time is also common to us on earth. Time is a teacher because it allows you to experience and to learn about things which are not available within other dimensions. When life seems to be dancing merrily along and you have managed to fit all the things into your day that you want to, then you may see time as your best friend. But when there never seems to be enough hours in the day, time may appear to be your enemy and something to be fought with. However, your soul guides you with just the right amount of time for any lifetime to teach you many of the lessons you need to learn.

222/6

Make Yourself Available

Everyone chooses times when they allow themselves to be available to life. For example, you may run your own business which sells clothes, and your passion for what you do drives you to work long hours, sometimes well into the night. However, it is you who has chosen to make yourself available to develop your career. Alternatively, you may be someone who spends all their time with a lover, or with their children, and again your availability is directed their way. When you open yourself up to life and your energy flows freely in a direction, these are the areas which you may need to be working on and learning about. Today, be aware of how you spend your energy, and if you choose you can learn to balance your availability in many directions.

223/7

Heaven And Earth

At times in your life you may find that you get too pre-occupied with material and earthly issues. For example, you may constantly worry about paying the mortgage, or worry about what you look like to the point of distraction, and so on. Sometimes the tables may turn and you may find yourself drifting off into the 'spirit world', and losing your earthly connection for a while. The spirit world is found deep inside you, as is your inner spiritual connection to the whole of humanity. The essential ingredients of life are both heaven and earth. Learn to be aware of how these aspects can be brought into balance in your life.

224/8

Building Dreams

When you have a dream which you want to build, holding the vision in your mind is indeed the most important step in creating your vision in reality. This is because holding your vision enables you to formulate a picture or a sense in your mind of how things 'should' be, and anybody involved with materializing your dream will sense this subconsciously. Of course, the fine details in your vision may alter slightly. For example, if you are an architect and are laying out plans for a new museum, then you hold the vision in your mind long before laying plans to paper. As the building work begins, you may redesign your plans several times in order to satisfy your vision. Learn to be aware of crafting and fine-tuning your life in order to help materialize your vision.

225/9

Break Out Of The Mould

People generally feel safe within their own boundaries. When situations occur to challenge these limits, they may feel very uncomfortable and nervous. For example, perhaps your family is very rich and you marry somebody materially poor (yet they are the answer to your dreams), and this ruffles their feathers. Or perhaps you may be distressed that your mother has, for example, decided to sell all her belongings and travel the world at the age of 75, and this shakes your foundations. When people do things or say things which appear 'out of character' others may desperately try to persuade them to do otherwise. Today, let go of living in any mould and learn to be adaptable to change and to life.

244

226/1

Vanity

Self-love is a wonderful attribute to develop; that is love for the soul and love and respect for your physical body, both of which are needed in this life. However, if you overemphasize the importance of your appearance, this may be because you feel an inner lack of love, or perhaps even a sense of worthlessness. Perhaps you are by everyone's opinion very beautiful or handsome. You may attract many people to you, but perhaps not everyone can stand you looking in the mirror every few minutes or dusting your face with make-up all the time. You may also hold an exaggerated opinion as to your own self-importance and people may at times back away from you. Learn to be aware of allowing the real you, the inner you, to shine through, no matter what you look like.

227/2

Why Worry?

People often spend a lot of time and energy worrying – about things which have happened, are happening, or about things which may never happen (although incessant worrying may actually contribute towards creating these very situations). Perhaps you spend time worrying about what other people think of you, but that is fruitless because everyone you know has a different opinion, and indeed what others think about you is none of your business at all! When you worry your energy is draining away. Today, learn to let go of worrying and take action to do something positive and constructive with your time instead.

228/3

The Warrior

Do you often look for issues and things in life to niggle or fight over? Perhaps you may think that this gives you something to do with your otherwise uneventful time, or even that it gives you some motivation, in a funny sort of way. Everyone has this warrior within themselves, however, and it may help you to acknowledge that it is there; perhaps then you can give up the fight. Indeed, instead of possessing a body which is always ready for a fight you can adopt a fighting spirit which can help you to get on with your life in a positive way. Your spirit doesn't fight but is fiery energy which can, like a match, create life from a single spark. Today, be aware of your inner spiritual warrior rearing up from within and learn to direct this energy in a positive way.

229/4

A Game Of Cricket

Life is like playing cricket with friends. You first find a group of friends (Soul Mates) whom you would like to play with and ask them if you can join their game. Then you try out different roles within the group (different relationships and experiences). For example, at one point you are batting and at other times you are bowling. Sometimes you are running and then you find yourself standing still waiting for some action to move in your direction (and you may even snooze off if the sun shines your way). At the end of each game you grow rich in knowledge from experience, and you have tales to tell your children and grandchildren, to pass on your wisdom to future participants who wish to play the game (of life).

230/5

Life Is Like A Maze

Mazes are fun when you know your way around them, and you have a map which directs you forward so that you do not get lost. Life is like a maze, and we are subconsciously finding our way around the map which has been all planned out. Sometimes you lose your way, but synchronicity prevails; perhaps being lost is what was meant to happen because you may then reorientate yourself completely. Being lost can also be fun as you muddle your way through (particularly if you are normally an organized person, in which case it may feel like a relief!). Every moment you are creating your own map of the world according to your own needs, and what may seem like a maze to others may be very clear to you.

231/6

Life Is What You Make It

You may try to run away from this simple fact but life really is what you make it. For example, you may be married and having affairs with three other partners at the same time, and wonder why your primary relationship isn't delivering what you want. But this is what you have contributed towards creating in your life, and if your energy is dispersed between many different partners then this is no surprise; life is what you make it. However, your soul teaches you the lessons you need and your ego joins in the learning process too. Today, take a look around you and notice the things that are working and those that are not, and take responsibility for your actions and what you intend to create.

232/7

Learn To Fly

Allow your mind to fly like an aeroplane and reach the sun, the moon and the stars, to connect with your innermost dreams, and then when you bring your ideas back to Earth, take a good look at them. You can take them apart, put them back together again, and examine every crumb of evidence. By the time everything has been liquidized and purified, the essence of what you have learned has been absorbed into your mind, body and spirit, and you can utilize this knowledge wisely if you choose. Your mind is free to roam about, and at any time it brings back essential information from its travels which can help you with your life. Your mind is a messenger, but like an e-mail box, it is up to you to pick up your messages, or to click in the right space for the information you need for today.

233/8

A New Address Book

At the end of each year you may go out and buy a new diary for the following year, but less often you may change address books. Perhaps you wait until your old one is bursting at the seams before you renew it, or you may have different address books – one for friends and family and one for business contacts. Buying a new address book gives you a valuable opportunity to connect with those who are in your life now. Some names you may re-enter into your new book whilst others may be left out because you have outgrown these relationships and you have all moved on. Composing a new address book can therefore be a wonderful time to re-evaluate your life. As you go through, perhaps you can thank all its participants for the lessons you have learned from each other.

234/9

Don't Interfere

As humans, we are at times prone to interfere with life. For example, perhaps we want to recover quickly from influenza so we take lots of vitamins. Of course, vitamins and minerals are essential for good health, but in this case, perhaps your body was just aching for a good sleep or a rest. Carrying on working whilst popping pills may help you in the short term, but perhaps your exhaustion gets worse and you very shortly end up spending even longer in bed as a result – your influenza may return. Perhaps you interfere with a situation at home; your brother and parents aren't on speaking terms and you try to bridge the gap and force the situation. Life has its own methods for working itself out, and in the end nature has its say anyway.

235/9

Use Your Diary

Each of your lifetimes is but a single page in a diary, and in it are lists of things to do and appointments for you to attend. Sometimes your diary gets too full and the task of completing what you need to do may seem impossible and your time on Earth may appear to go very slowly indeed. Whilst on subsequent pages (in other lifetimes) you may have very few entries – whoopee! holidays! A diary is, of course, a guideline, and although you have things you need to accomplish, at the end of the day you have the choice and you can refuse to address these things – but they may come back to haunt you at a later date. You may also add things in at the last minute. Today, you may like to aim to accomplish all the most important things on your agenda, if you can.

236/2

Love Hearts

Have you found your love heart, and opened your heart to life to let the love in? To find your love heart, all you need to do is look within, and to love what you find (even when you ain't no saint at times). The more you are able to love yourself, the easier it is to share your love with your own special love heart, that sweetie pie who lights up your life, your own lover or mate. Love is a very freeing energy because it allows you to feel all your emotions and teaches you to love yourself, and to love others for who they are. Love hearts are all around you because your soul knows the true nature of love, and recognizing that everyone has a heart may help to open you up to using yours too.

237/3

Get A Life

Sensitivity to your soul is a wonderful quality to possess; you can feel what it is teaching you. Sometimes you may also be too sensitive and hide from people for a while whilst dreaming your life away. You may, for example, be blessed with good health, but since you sprained your ankle you become reclusive and dreamy. Perhaps you hide away because you are hurt by all the comments people make about you hobbling around in bandages, or because you may feel awkward and out of place, even though everyone is fussing around you and lavishing you with love and attention. However, the saying 'get a life' means being who you are, and learning from all the experiences you go through in your life, even when you are being over-sensitive and dreamy at times too.

238/4

Do You Fly Off The Handle?

When you are sailing along in life and everything is calm, and your horizon shows sunshine and a silky sea ahead, then you may be more likely to 'fly off the handle' if the boat breaks down or when a freak waves almost turns your boat upside down. But it is at these very times when you can apply your innermost calm to help you sort out these situations for the best. For example, by flying off the handle when your boss refuses to give you a pay rise, you may give him or her the excuse to reiterate their belief that you do not deserve it, in addition to other reasons. Indeed, you may have reacted to the news of the moment, but choosing to take a calm view may have persuaded your boss to give in to you. Today, learn to hold the wheel steady so that you keep the peace.

239/5

Chill Out

When you find yourself knee-deep in commitments – with a partner, family, friends, work and life – and you feel like you just can't take any more, then it may be time to take a breather and just chill out. You might have a relaxing massage, go for a swim, spend a day in bed with your lover, or exit to the nearest beach and fall asleep under a canopy with a stiff drink in one hand and a magazine in the other. Chilling out means that when you do return to your regular routine you can inject more energy into it because you are refreshed. Perhaps you find that at least some of your pressures may have just melted away and others have taken a back seat to your new-found vitality. Making a commitment to chill out regularly may also help you with your whole life.

240/6

Do Your Duty

Doing your duty sometimes seems like sacrificing your own needs and desires to help or please others. For example, your parents have paid a lot of money to send you to one of the top schools around. Halfway through the training you may want to duck out because you feel you have chosen the wrong course, but you feel it is your duty to finish what you started because your parents have paid for you. However, your soul makes up a contract with you in order for you to learn important lessons in life, and taking responsibility for yourself and learning about duty are some of them. So although you think it is your parents whom you feel dutiful towards, they are simply mirrors of your soul reminding you of this lesson.

241/7

Green

The colours in your environment play a leading role in your life. Colours are energies which vibrate at different wavelengths; some of these you may strongly resonate with and others may not attract you. You may wear one colour – red for example – for a long time, and then switch off from wearing it. The colour green, which is at the middle of the colour spectrum, is believed to have a wonderful balancing influence on most people. When you are feeling hyperactive, for example, it can help to calm you down; and if you are low in energy it can help to relax, and even energize, you. This may be why the colour green is found so extensively in nature – because nature is constantly performing a balancing act.

242/8

The Good Life

Everyone can enjoy the good life. It's not dependent upon how much money you have or upon those around you; it is based on the simple things in life. That is, self-love (of your body and soul), a love and respect for others, and an appreciation for life. Indeed, the most simple things in life are free. Have you ever, for example, found yourself going through a busy, demanding phase, and realized that all you really needed was to switch off and find time to be? Perhaps you would like to go for a walk, eat a simple meal, spend time with a partner or a few close friends, not answer the telephone for a while, and so on. Nature is simple – the sun rises and falls, the moon lights your way, the seasons come and go – and keeping life simple is often the best way.

243/9

The Lighthouse

When you are feeling sensitive or are going through great changes in your life, find the light so that it can help to show you the way. Lighthouses are found near the coastline, and shine bright beacons of light to help guide ships and sea vessels to safety. Light is the most powerful source of life on this planet and can over-ride even the darkest times you may go through in your life. You can look outside yourself for the light if you choose, but in effect you needn't look far because your greatest source of strength is the light deep within you. Know that your inner light is always shining, and learn to seek guidance from within.

244/1

Find Your Passion

Some people have a passion for life. They dive in fully and make the most out of everything that comes their way. Although, like everyone, they experience challenges in their lives, they dust themselves off and carry on, and perhaps try not to take life too seriously. Others may find life itself a challenge and struggle to keep going. To them, it seems like there are endless situations to face, and at times they feel they have barely enough strength to carry on. Finding and expressing those things you feel passionate about, however, can help to keep the fires burning, and make you feel good being alive. Perhaps you are passionate about golf, for example, and when you play your eyes light up, and your whole mind, body and spirit aligns. Learn to find the passions that keep you alive and kicking.

245/2

Physical Changes Come From Spirit

Changes which occur in your life at the physical level all come from spirit because it is at this level that bigger decisions about your life are made. For example, perhaps your soul and spirit guide you to end a relationship after many years because it is no longer serving you (your partner has also expressed these to be his or her wishes). You may fuss or fight, try to resist the process and battle with the decision, which you know you need to make, thus prolonging the pain. But giving in to changes which are the best for all concerned helps you to move forwards with your life in a positive way. The more in tune you are with your inner self, the easier it may be for you to see 'warning signs' in any area of your life, which can sometimes help you avoid conflicts later on.

246/3

Your Natural Inheritance

Some skills and attributes you inherit from your parents, grandparents and past generations, and other things you develop as time goes on. For example, you may have a brilliant gift for making things out of wood with your hands (as did your grandfather), but when you are 32 you develop a gift for playing the piano, even though nobody has been musical in your family. This new skill may be part of your karmic inheritance. Some gifts you may also not feel comfortable using because they get you in contact with situations from the past. Today, be aware that who you are is your natural inheritance, although whether you use your gifts is your choice.

247/4

You Are A Survivor

Your soul and spirit know the best time for you to be born to utilize your best potential. They also know the best time for you to die – when you have completed the major lessons you need to learn. Of course, you can opt out of lessons and decide to have a holiday, or opt out of life by running away from your obligations. You are a survivor, and the fact that you are alive means that you have great potential: things for you to do, people to see, experiences to have. The art of being a survivor is perhaps your ability to look ahead to the things that you would like or need to do. These can be simple things like looking forward to getting up and eating breakfast each day, or greater things like climbing Mount Everest, and so on.

248/5

Mission Statement

We are all representatives of the space and time we live in. Space, which contains the unforeseen, makes up perhaps 80 per cent of the great unknown; time is the dimension our little planet is governed by, and the year in which we live. We as humans are all on a mission, and together all the nations of the Earth are defining and redefining our Mission Statement, and each generation adapts and refines it a little more to suit what's needed. Indeed, if the majority agree on what our statement is, we can continue to carry the world forward in a positive way, knowing that we collectively take responsibility for what we are creating around us.

249/6

Soul Opportunities

At the level of the soul, everyone has equal amounts of opportunities for personal development work, change and growth, but it is up to us to develop and go for our potential. For example, we may be born in completely different countries and circumstances, but we can work with what we do have, which on a soul level is perfect for us. Perhaps you live in India and grow food on a small patch of land, and this helps your own family to survive as well as providing for nearby villagers. On a soul level, your lesson may be to learn about sharing, which of course you do by willingly sharing what you do have with those around you. Today, be aware of your opportunities for growth from your soul and your ego or personality's point of view.

250/7

Synchronicity Prevails

Synchronicity means that you may travel to the other side of the world and bump into your next-door neighbours who are residing at the same hotel. Perhaps you go out to dinner together and get to chat about issues which you wouldn't normally consider talking to each other about. This is synchronicity at play, which gives you a gentle reminder that we are all connected and there's no getting away from synchronicity. You may realize that, ultimately, everything happens for a reason, and by being open you can read the 'writing on the wall', and learn from the messages that life is sending you.

Further Reading

There are so many Numerology books on the market today that everyone's taste is catered for – Numerology for your lover, family, friends, children and work colleagues, Numerology and your health, Numerology and your career, Numerology for your soul and for the world at large. Each of these wonderful books can give you the opportunity to grow and learn more about life through the jewels of information they reveal.

It is your inner wisdom which guides you to choose the best possible Numerology books for you. However, here is one specific book which I can highly recommend:

Faith Javane and Dusty Bunker, *Numerology and The Divine Triangle*, Whitford Press, USA, 1979.

This book marries both authors' extensive knowledge of Numerology, Astrology and the Tarot, and is a true masterpiece of its time. It encompasses the fact that all knowledge reveals the truth at its core, whatever disciplines are used. This book is practical and easily readable for the beginner; it highlights the Numerology of your date of birth and names. It is also a companion for any Numerologist who wishes to understand more about the Pythagorian method. Altogether an inspiring personal development book.

BOOKS BY SONIA DUCIE
- The Principles of Numerology
- Do It Yourself Numerology
- Numerology: Your Love and Relationship Guide
- Numerology: Your Personal Guide for Life
- The Complete Illustrated Guide to Numerology
- The Self Help Reflexology Handbook

Useful Addresses

If you would like to contact a Numerology school or association to find out about professional training and workshops, or to find a professional Numerologist for a chart reading, please send a stamped SAE or international reply coupon to:

UNITED KINGDOM
The Secretary
Association Internationale de Numerologues (A.I.N.)
8 Melbourn Street
Royston
Hertfordshire SG8 7BZ

Connaissance School of Numerology
Royston Cave, Art and Book Shop
8 Melbourn Street
Royston
Hertfordshire
SG8 7BZ

FRANCE
Christian Gilles School
Residence de L'Abbey Royle
17 Rue Pirel
93200 Saint Denis
Paris

AUSTRALIA
Character Analysis and Numerology
Mrs C. Anschutz
23 Flinders Street
Kent Town
5067
South Australia

NEW ZEALAND
Francie Williams
North Shore Parapsychology School
60 East Coast Bay Road
Milford
New Zealand

USA
Marina D. Graham
888 Prospect Street
La Jolla
Suite 200
CA 92037